TABLE OF CONTENTS

EXECUTIVE SUMMARY

Introduction

In November 1999, the U.S. Congress passed the National Park System New Area Study Act of 2000 (S. 1349) as contained in Public Law 106-113, Appendix C, "National Park Service Studies Act of 1999." The act instructed the Secretary of the Interior "to direct special resource studies to determine the national significance of the sites, and/or areas, listed in Section 5 of this Act to determine the national significance of each site, and/or area, as well as the suitability and feasibility of their inclusion as units of the National Park System." Among the areas to be studied were "Civil Rights Sites" on a "multi-state" level.

As part of its National Historic Landmarks program, the National Park Service in partnership with the Organization of American Historians (OAH) prepared this civil rights framework study to assist the National Park Service in identifying and prioritizing those areas of history significant in illustrating the civil rights story. Implementation of the framework's recommendations will help planners evaluate proposals by Congress and others for additions to both the National Park System and the National Trails System, and will also assist the responsible authorities in states, federal agencies, and Indian tribes to identify sites for National Historic Landmarks designation.

The period of significance for the study begins in 1776, when Thomas Jefferson wrote in the Declaration of Independence that "all men are created equal." The period ends in 1976, to include the growing civil rights movements of several minority groups in the dozen years following the passage of the Civil Rights Act of 1964.

Before 1776, certainly, the rights of enslaved people, women, American Indians, and immigrants such as the Scots-Irish were routinely violated within the boundaries of the present United States, especially with respect to personal liberty, voting, educational opportunities, property ownership, and religious affiliation. During this period, however, such rights were subject not only to the laws of the mother country but also to the laws and judicial interpretations of the several colonies, some of which took a more liberal approach than did others. There was no national government to define or ensure civil rights, much less a national consensus about what those rights were. It was not until 1776 that a clear statement regarding civil rights rang out, in the words of the Declaration: "We hold these truths to be self-evident: That all men are created equal; that they are endowed by their Creator with certain inalienable rights; that among these are life, liberty, and the pursuit of happiness." Although Thomas Jefferson's words have sometimes seemed to ring hollow, they nonetheless constitute one of America's shining ideals—an inspiration to the world—that all citizens have equal rights and stand equal before the law.

Almost two centuries later, the preamble of another great document, the Civil Rights Act of 1964, clearly stated as its purpose the guarantee of the principles enunciated in the Declaration. Congress passed the act "to enforce the constitutional right to vote, to confer jurisdiction upon the district courts of the United States to provide injunctive relief against discrimination in public accommodations, to authorize the Attorney General to institute suits to protect constitutional rights in public facilities and public education, to extend the Commission on Civil Rights, to prevent discrimination in federally assisted programs, to establish a Commission on Equal Employment Opportunity, and for other purposes." Although the protected parties were defined somewhat differently in individual sections of the act, generally they included all citizens without regard to "race, color, religion, sex, or national origin." Subsequent interpretations of the act have applied the equal protection principle regardless of sexual orientation. The provisions of the act relating to the right to vote, access to public accommodations, public education, and equal employment opportunity (in the private sector as well as in federal government employment) serve as themes within the Civil Rights Framework. In 1990, the Americans with Disabilities Act extended the "powers, remedies, and procedures" of the Civil Rights Act of 1964 to disabled Americans to prohibit discrimination in employment, public accommodations, and other matters.

Methodology

The National Park Service worked with OAH scholars to produce a historical overview placing civil rights within the context of U.S. history for women, African Americans, American Indians, Hispanics, Asian Americans, and gays and lesbians. As the work proceeded, the scholars used the overview to identify themes other than those derived from the Civil Rights Act of 1964. These themes included immigrant rights, criminal injustice, and the American Indian nations' struggle to retain their sovereignty, lands, rights, and culture. The historians also identified examples of civil rights events, places, and individuals that are included in the framework's overview. In the 2008 revision, the National Park Service added certain events to the scholars' examples to include the founding of the NAACP and important events in Asian American history. Using this information, National Park Service historians and planners determined the representation of civil rights-related sites in the National Historic Landmarks program and in National Park System units. Based on the historical overview and an analysis of existing civil rights-related sites, the study makes the following findings and conclusions.

Study Findings

This study found that the National Park Service has both identified and interpreted many nationally significant civil rights sites and that further study is needed to identify other civil rights sites associated with events, places, and people the scholars identified as important to the national story.

1. **Many civil rights-related sites have been identified and recognized.** The current status of the National Park Service's civil rights story is most readily reflected in prominent individuals such as Susan B. Anthony and Martin Luther King, Jr., and well-known events like the desegregation of Little Rock Central High School and the 1965 Selma-to-Montgomery Voting Rights March. Most sites represent the lifetime work of activists or pivotal moments in civil rights history. Of the National Historic Landmarks identified in Table 1, thirty-three are associated with African Americans, sixteen with American Indians, fifteen with women, six with Asian Americans, one with Hispanics, and one with the gay and lesbian movement. National Park Service units and National Historic Trails that interpret civil rights include nine associated with African Americans, three with American Indians, two with women, and two with Asian Americans.

2. **A number of civil rights-related sites have not been recognized.** The historians who contributed to this study listed many events, places, and people in the overview that are not yet evaluated within a theme study. This list is not intended to be comprehensive or definitive, but to help National Park Service assess how well civil rights sites are represented. Regarding the various minority groups, the inventory of civil rights sites is limited for Hispanics and Asian Americans, and American Indians in the New Deal (1934-1945), Termination (1945-1960), and Self-Determination (1960-1975) eras. In regard to historical themes, however, the National Park Service is addressing the topics of public accommodations, equal employment, housing, and voting within theme studies.

Study Recommendations

Because some areas of civil rights are underrepresented in interpreting our cultures, this study recommends completing four National Historic Landmark theme studies to recognize, promote, and protect civil rights-related sites that meet the National Park Service's thematic framework of "creating social institutions and movements" and "shaping the political landscape." Theme studies assist park planners and historians in identifying sites that may be considered for preservation within the National Park System and National Historic Landmark designation.

1. **Complete chapters of the National Historic Landmarks theme study: *Civil Rights in America*.** Based on the four provisions of the 1960s civil rights acts (voting, equal employment, housing, and public accommodations), the *Civil Rights in America* theme study portrays chapters in the nation's civil rights story, each having its own significance within the movement. Every chapter provides a historic context, registration guidelines, and a National Historic Landmark study list of properties that have strong associations with nationally significant topics within the civil rights context. Two draft chapters currently available are *Desegregation of Public Accommodations* and *Racial Voting Rights*. The final two chapters in preparation are *Racial Discrimination in Housing* and *Racial Employment Discrimination*. The *Civil Rights in America* theme study accompanies the previously completed theme study, *Racial Desegregation in Public Education in the United States* (2000), a study that has produced eight National Historic Landmark designations.

2. **Subject to available funding, undertake civil rights studies related to other minority groups.** The framework study examined topics related to the history of other minority groups within the United States, including Asian Americans, Hispanics, gays and lesbians, and women, as well as the unique American Indian civil rights story (including Alaska Natives and Native Hawaiians). Undertaking additional studies will assist National Park Service units with telling the civil rights story related to these groups and identify related sites and individuals relevant to these groups for possible National Historic Landmark nomination.

THE CIVIL RIGHTS FRAMEWORK STUDY

CIVIL RIGHTS – Those rights guaranteed to an individual as a member of society.[1]

INTRODUCTION

In 1964 Congress adopted the most comprehensive civil rights legislation in United States history. The Civil Rights Act of 1964 (1) guaranteed all Americans the right to vote; (2) prohibited discrimination in public accommodations based on race, color, religion, or national origin; (3) outlawed job discrimination on the basis of race, color, religion, sex, or national origin; and (4) gave the federal government broad authority in enforcement. The civil rights movement leading up to this act was "one of the most publicized events in United States history. Short of a declaration of war, no other act of Congress had a more violent background—a background of confrontation, official violence, injury, and murder that has few parallels in American history."[2]

The issue of who is guaranteed legal equality has been contested by women, minority groups, congresses, and federal courts ever since Thomas Jefferson asserted in the Declaration of Independence that "all men are created equal." Clearly, the evolution of our present understanding of civil rights is deeply tied to our collective story and represents the highest aspirations and deepest tragedies that followed the adoption of our national charter. It is wholly within the mission of the National Park Service to locate, evaluate, recognize, preserve, and interpret nationally significant sites associated with the many threads of the civil rights story.

The National Park Service has identified a number of civil rights-related resources, some of which have been established as units of the National Park System. Still others have been designated as National Historic Landmarks. To identify and interpret other related sites, the National Park Service must consider the site's relationship to the civil rights story's chronology, historical themes, and how various minorities are represented. The National Park Service has partnered with the Organization of American Historians (OAH) to provide an overview of civil rights history, and a list of people, events, and places that tell the story. Participating OAH historians are identified in the Contributors section of this framework.

This framework study identifies broad themes within the civil rights story, as well as the events, persons, and places that represent those themes, and assesses the degree to which related sites are represented and recognized. The framework will enable the National Park Service to decide which themes and minority groups need further intensive study to identify and evaluate nationally significant sites. Implementing the framework will allow planners to evaluate proposals by Congress and others to add units to the National Park System, establish National Historic Trails, and recognize sites through National Historic Landmark designation.

---

[1] William Safire, *Safire's New Political Dictionary* (New York: Random House, 1993), 127.
[2] Robert D. Loevy, ed., *The Civil Rights Act of 1964: The Passage of the Law That Ended Racial Segregation* (Albany: State University of New York Press, 1997), 40, 42.

OVERVIEW OF CIVIL RIGHTS HISTORY

MOVEMENT: The activities of a group of people to achieve a goal.[3]

TELLING THE STORY

This overview describes the efforts of women and minority groups to secure and enforce civil rights under the U.S. Constitution. The minority groups include American Indians, African Americans, Hispanics, Asian Americans, and gays and lesbians. Their struggles shaped the Civil Rights Act of 1964, and its provisions (equal employment, public accommodations, voting, and equal education) serve as major themes of the civil rights story both before and after the act's passage. Other themes—less directly associated with the Civil Rights Act than the enumerated provisions but of equal historical importance—include immigrant rights, criminal injustice, and the American Indian nations' struggle to retain their sovereignty, lands, rights, and culture.

The level of information for each minority group in this historical overview is mainly dependent on two factors: whether the civil rights story of a minority group is documented and how closely related their story is to the themes. The best-known instance of denial of civil rights and the struggle to have them made effective was the resistance of southern states to the principle of blacks having equal rights with whites. By comparison, the history of civil rights for Hispanics is far less developed. Only within the past thirty years have specialists recovered the long-neglected history of Hispanic people in the United States. Their historical record on some subjects such as public accommodations and equal employment is much less developed than for education and voting rights. Many books have been published in recent years that treat civil rights issues within broader themes of Hispanic culture and history.

Similarly, the history of civil rights for Asian Americans has not been well publicized, but like that of other minorities, it is an important chapter in civil rights history. Few people know, for example, the critical contributions of Asian Americans to the development of the concept of citizenship in the United States. Asian Americans as a whole have faced harassment and discrimination in various forms, from brutal physical violence to obstacles in such areas as education, employment, and housing. Other important aspects of Asian American civil rights history are related to immigration and World War II internment. Cultural and ethnic diversity characterizes "Asian America," and often one national group's civil rights experience has been substantially different from that of other groups. Although relatively few books have been published solely on the subject of Asian American civil rights history, in recent years many books have addressed civil rights issues within broader themes of Asian American culture and history.

The gay, lesbian, bisexual, and transgender movement began to emerge in the 1950s. Because people involved in same-sex relationships faced execution during the early years of the Republic, and ridicule, abuse, and discrimination thereafter, they long suppressed their stories. By the mid-twentieth century, individuals and groups of gays and lesbians had begun asserting a right to public space, but as a form of cultural rather than political resistance. They also formed a variety of organizations to fight for justice and improve their lives. Of all the minority groups, only this

---

[3] *Webster's II New Riverside University Dictionary* (Boston: The Houghton Mifflin Company), 1988.

one required a political act—coming out—for its members to be identifiable. Their civil rights history includes police harassment in public places and employment discrimination in government, schools, and the military.

The civil rights struggle for women is a window on changing definitions of citizenship and the ways it has been shaped by gender, race, and class. Because women constitute half of every racial, ethnic, religious, or regional group, their story is difficult to tell in isolation. The clearest narratives are found in the campaign for the right to vote and the subsequent debates over the Equal Rights Amendment. Although educated, predominately white, and mostly middle-class women led the various movements, success depended on coalitions and alliances with working-class and minority women. It is important to tell this story in a way that renders visible the full diversity of the participants and links the women's civil rights struggles to those of other groups and to clarify the different perspectives and priorities that profoundly affect the implicit meanings of that ambiguous word "equality."

Very little has also been recorded about American Indian protests against discrimination in public accommodations, education, voting rights, and employment. Not all American Indian experiences fit the "civil rights" model. Rather, American Indians dealt with white racism while trying to define their individual rights vis-à-vis their own tribal governments, which makes their civil rights movement unique among minority groups. American Indians faced intense federal pressures to assimilate into white society while struggling to maintain their freedom, lands, and ways of life. Issues of sovereignty, treaty rights, land restoration, economic development, burial rights, and religious freedom define their movement. A wide variety of books has been published about American Indian history and culture that also discuss civil rights-related issues.

The following overview is separated into chronological sections that identify phases in the development of civil rights between 1776 and 1976. Each section contains brief descriptions of women and minority experiences submitted by the OAH historians, as well as their lists of at least five to ten people, places, and events that they judge to be of national significance. Parts 1 through 6 discuss the experience of women and all minorities. Part 7 discusses the American Indian Movement and the unique civil rights experience of these people. These descriptions are placed within the political, social, or economic aspects of the time period to complete the overview.

PART 1. AN EMERGING CAUSE, 1776–1865

The Declaration of Independence declared that "all men are created equal," and in 1788, the U.S. Constitution purported to "secure the blessings of liberty" to the American people. These rights and liberties, however, were meant only for white men of property. The Founding Fathers never imagined that women, African Americans (both slave and free), or men without property could be the equal of the propertied white men entrusted with participation in the civic arena. Nonwhite men who were of other than African descent were also excluded, as Congress had stipulated in the Naturalization Act of 1790 that only "free white persons" could become citizens. Ironically, the majority of white males who became naturalized citizens between 1830 and 1860 enjoyed manhood suffrage and other rights denied to native-born nonwhites.

Crusaders against slavery and racism advanced the concept of equality before the law, regardless of race, and often quoted the Declaration of Independence to condemn the institution of slavery that evolved after the first Africans landed involuntarily at Jamestown, Virginia, in 1619. Many abolitionists searched for color-blind citizenship, while slavery proponents viewed nonwhites as inferior races unworthy of Constitutional rights. Women abolitionists of the 1830s and 1840s initiated their own movement in the 1840s; one rooted in an emerging white middle class and women's traditional roles in creating a civil society. Their civic duty, as captured in the phrase "Republican motherhood," was to raise virtuous citizens (sons) and to encourage their husbands to exercise civic virtues. Pushing against the boundaries of their so-called "separate sphere," women began to challenge the assigned roles of men and women in civic life, as well as access to the duties of citizenship.

Nineteenth-century territorial expansion raised civil rights issues among those who lost their lands and for new immigrants seeking economic prosperity. Mexicans who supposedly gained their constitutional rights of citizenship after the U.S. takeover of the Southwest confronted disputes in race wars, lynchings, murders, and the application of unequal justice that lasted into the early twentieth century. Chinese workers who arrived after the discovery of gold in California marked the first major wave of Asian immigration to America. Those who followed them from other Asian countries, such as Japan, Korea, and India, added a dynamic dimension to the racial diversity of American society. In comparison with African Americans, Asian Americans were not enslaved, although some were virtual "wage slaves." Because they were nonwhite, however, they were denied many civil rights granted white European immigrants, including political and economic rights. They were, in other words, "between black and white."

Within American society, nontraditional relationships were not tolerated. People involved in same-sex relationships or those who crossed the gender line were threatened with execution, imprisonment, or other forms of punishment for gathering in public places, engaging in sexual activity, or cross-dressing in public.

Examples of civil rights events and individuals

Abigail Adams, the wife of President John Adams, urged better legal treatment of women before and after the American Revolution.

National Negro Conventions were held beginning in the 1830s. These periodic meetings of leading blacks organized the race's protests against slavery and discrimination and devised plans and programs for racial advancement. The meetings foreshadowed later African American civil rights and self-help organizations.

Richard Allen of Philadelphia was the first national black leader in the United States. A founder of the Free African Society in 1787 and the African Methodist Episcopal (AME) Church in 1793, the race's first self-help and independent institutions, he was also the president of the National Negro Convention.

Frederick Douglass gained fame as an antislavery orator and writer. During the Civil War, he galvanized black support for the military effort, and afterwards was the nation's chief spokesperson for civil rights. Starting in 1847, he published the weekly newspaper *The North Star*, which promoted abolitionism, African American rights, women's rights, and a host of related reforms.

Sarah and Angelina Grimké were sisters who were 1830s Southern abolitionist pioneers.

Woman's Rights Convention, held in Seneca Falls, New York, in 1848, formally began the women's struggle for equality. Such meetings would be held almost annually up to the onset of the Civil War.

Elizabeth Cady Stanton initiated the suffragist movement and at the Woman's Rights Convention, wrote the Declaration of Sentiments that called for a broad array of rights for women.

The Elizabeth Cady Stanton Home Women's Rights National Historical Park
National Park Service Photograph

Lucretia Mott was a women's suffrage organizer who, with Elizabeth Cady Stanton, agreed at the 1840 World Anti-Slavery Convention to plan the first women's rights convention, which was held in Seneca Falls in 1848.

Sojourner Truth was a former slave who became a national symbol for strong black women and an advocate of women's and blacks' rights.

Roberts v. City of Boston was an 1849 Massachusetts Supreme Court decision that established the "separate but equal" doctrine in a public school segregation case.

People v. Hall was an 1854 Supreme Court of California ruling that Chinese people, like blacks and Indians, could not give testimony in court against whites.

PART 2. RECONSTRUCTION AND REPRESSION, 1865–1900

In 1865, following the Civil War, southern state legislatures began enacting Black Codes to restrict freedmen's rights and maintain the plantation system. The Republican-controlled Congress responded to these measures between 1866 and 1870 by passing the three great postwar constitutional amendments (Thirteenth, Fourteenth, and Fifteenth) that abolished slavery, guaranteed the newly freed blacks equal protection of the laws, and gave all male American citizens the right to vote regardless of their "race, color, or previous condition of servitude." Congress also passed the Civil Rights Acts of 1866 and 1875 to protect the rights of all Americans (excluding Indians) regardless of race. Henceforth, all persons born in the U.S. were national citizens with rights to "the full and equal enjoyment" of public places, among other rights. Freedmen and other persons of color looked forward to asserting their political rights and receiving equal treatment before the law, but they were soon disappointed.

As Reconstruction came to an end in 1877, the concept of equal rights collapsed in the wake of legislative and judicial actions. The Republican and Democratic parties sacrificed civil rights in exchange for white southern votes. In the *Civil Rights Cases* of 1883, the U.S. Supreme Court found the statutory guarantee of equal enjoyment of public accommodations unconstitutional on the grounds that the equal protection clause of the Fourteenth Amendment only applied to state activities and did not permit federal control of individual actions. This decision greatly limited the rights of blacks and strengthened Jim Crow laws in the South.

The passage of the Fourteenth and Fifteenth Amendments was partly responsible for the singular focus of women's rights activists on the right to vote. The enfranchisement of African American men, which many women supported, in effect embedded into the Constitution a gender-based definition of citizenship and divided the women's rights activists in the northern and midwestern states who had been part of the abolition movement. For some, guaranteeing only black men the right to vote was a necessary compromise at the end of a long and incredibly bloody war. For others, it constituted a betrayal of the equal rights concept. For all the women who demanded civic equality, women's suffrage soon became the principal objective. It was also the most controversial goal because it constituted a direct claim to participation in public life.

Many of the restrictions that African Americans suffered, Asian Americans endured as well. They likewise were excluded from public life, isolated in segregated schools, and discriminated against in regard to employment and housing. They also suffered under bans on racial intermarriage and limitations on real property ownership. Unlike blacks, the Chinese were excluded from immigration after 1882, while many other Asians were limited in the numbers that could legally immigrate, and none were allowed to become citizens.

In the 1890s, Congress and the Supreme Court began redefining which minorities were entitled to citizenship. Congress began conferring citizenship status on Indians in certain states, albeit without full citizenship rights, such as the right to travel freely, manage their own money, vote (in some states), and purchase firearms and alcohol. In the case of the *United States v. Wong Kim Ark*, the Supreme Court ruled in 1898 that individuals born in the United States of Chinese parents could not be stripped of their American citizenship, which the Fourteenth Amendment guaranteed. This ruling upheld an important constitutional principle—persons born in America are citizens entitled to civil rights protections and due process—but state and federal courts and legislatures frequently ignored the civil rights and due process aspects of the amendment nonetheless.

Despite these partial successes, in 1896 the final devastating blow to the civil rights gains made during Reconstruction came in the form of judicially sanctioned segregation. In *Plessy v. Ferguson,* the U.S. Supreme Court affirmed the concept of separate but equal public facilities, thus ensuring racial segregation and discrimination, especially in education. Whites would use this concept to keep African Americans, as well as other minorities, in separate and unequal facilities.

The last decades of the nineteenth century were a time when vast and dramatic changes took place throughout America, many of them as a consequence of the Civil War. Urbanization, industrialization, immigration, the ferment of populism and labor struggles, the expansion of education, the settlement of the West and the end of the frontier, and the emergence of women's professions created a more diversified and complicated setting for the equal rights struggle. In the first years of the new century, these changes helped to inspire intensified civil rights efforts, particularly in the last phase of the women's suffrage movement.

Examples of civil rights events and individuals

Susan B. Anthony, who was active in numerous reform movements, entered the fight for women's rights in 1851. In 1869, she played the leading role in organizing the National Woman Suffrage Association, which focused on the passage of an amendment to the Constitution.

Ida B. Wells-Barnett led other African American women to mobilize their extensive networks of clubs and reform associations on behalf of women's suffrage despite exclusion from most white suffrage associations. By late in the nineteenth century, middle-class African American women had created an educational and civic infrastructure within the black community, especially clubs. They knew the empowering necessity of suffrage as they experienced the crushing repression of southern Jim Crow laws and the disfranchisement of African American men. Wells-Barnett also led a fiery international anti-lynching campaign that resulted in the founding of the Anti-Lynching Committee in 1893 while she was on a speaking tour of London.

The Women's Suffrage Movement achieved a milestone in 1890 when the Territory of Wyoming was admitted to the Union with its suffrage provision intact, becoming the first state with women suffrage.

Booker T. Washington made Tuskegee Institute in Alabama the most renowned institution for the higher education of blacks in the late nineteenth and early twentieth centuries with support from northern and southern industrialists and philanthropists. After his "Atlanta Compromise" address in 1895 that called for blacks to accept segregation in return for future economic opportunity, he emerged as the premiere national African American leader and held that title until the emergence of Martin Luther King, Jr., sixty years later.

The First Chinese Exclusion Act, which Congress passed in 1882, banned Chinese labor immigration for ten years (the period was later extended numerous times) and declared that Chinese immigrants could not become naturalized citizens. A significant event in Asian American history, the law is also a landmark event in the development of U.S. immigration laws. It was the first comprehensive immigration act of the nation and marked the beginning of the federal government's restrictive immigration policies. It was also the first law to ban immigration on the basis of race.

United States v. Wong Kim Ark resulted in a U.S. Supreme Court decision in 1898 that persons born in the United States of Chinese parents could not be stripped of their American citizenship, thereby reaffirming a vital legal principle established in the Fourteenth Amendment. Courts and legislatures continued, however, to ignore other aspects of the amendment's equal protection provisions.

The Visitor Center at Women's Rights National Historical Park
National Park Service photograph

PART 3. REKINDLING CIVIL RIGHTS, 1900-1941

Massive social and governmental changes took place in America in the first decades of the twentieth century, fueled by the Progressive Era, World War I, and the Great Depression. Efforts to combat discrimination found expression in biracial activism and reform movements. Hopes for equality soared for many minority groups, but most ended in grave disappointment.

The Progressive Era of 1900-1920 brought the largest electoral change in U.S. history. After a decades-long struggle, women gained voting rights under the Nineteenth Amendment in 1920. Despite the adoption of the amendment, however, black women as well as African American men in the South remained disfranchised, as they and poor whites and immigrants were denied or lost voting rights by state-imposed literacy tests and residency and registration requirements.

Military service and increased employment during World War I brought minorities new hopes for greater equality and economic opportunity. Activists argued that fighting to make the world safe for democracy and for the rights of the oppressed would dismantle racial inequality at home. After the war, however, black veterans encountered the same racial restrictions that were in place previously, and many of those who sought wartime job opportunities in the North faced the same discrimination that existed in the Jim Crow South. Hispanics who came to fill worker shortages were viewed merely as cheap labor. By the 1920s and 1930s, Hispanic Americans were fighting for decent wages and organizing farm workers.

After the stock market crash of 1929 and the beginning of the Great Depression, the federal government's New Deal programs offered opportunities for employment reform. Responding to charges that many blacks were the "last hired and first fired," the Roosevelt administration instituted changes that enabled people of all races to obtain needed job training and employment. These programs brought public works employment opportunities to African Americans, especially in the North. Roosevelt also advanced black interests by using his executive powers and avoiding the predominantly southern Democratic majorities of the House and Senate, and by creating the Civil Rights Section of the Justice Department. Those blacks who could vote began switching their party affiliation from Republican to Democrat, thereby becoming the first wave of black voters to shape social and political reform.

With the loss of voting rights and continued enforced segregation, minorities began to form organizations to litigate for their civil rights. Examples of such organizations included the National Association for the Advancement of Colored People (NAACP), established in 1909 (initiated as the Niagara Movement in 1905); the National Urban League in 1910; and the Congress of Spanish Speaking People in 1939.

Some organizations began launching legal challenges to segregated schools late in the 1930s. As with the racially segregated schools in the South, southwestern school districts systematically segregated Mexican children into so-called "Mexican schools" or "Mexican classrooms." The first precedent-setting local and state level court cases to desegregate Mexican and African American schooling were decided during this time.

The debate regarding citizenship for Asian immigrants and its accompanying rights continued. Asian immigrants faced changing immigration laws and remained ineligible for citizenship. Sixteen states denied land ownership, among other rights, to Asian Americans. Racial prejudice was reflected blatantly in a 1923 Supreme Court decision that Asian Indians as nonwhites were ineligible for U.S. citizenship, because although ample historical and anthropological evidence established their "whiteness," American society did not accept them as such.

Also during this time period, the gay and lesbian movement started taking shape. Social analysts began rejecting prior medical definitions of "inversion" or "homosexuality" as deviant. Communities of men and women with same-sex affiliations began to grow in urban areas. Their right to gather in public places such as bars was tenuous, and police raids and harassment were common.

Examples of civil rights events, places, and individuals

W. E. B. Du Bois was a major black leader in the first half of the twentieth century; a founding member in 1905 of the Niagara Movement, which later became the NAACP; editor of the NAACP's *Crisis* magazine; and a proponent of academic education for blacks (in contrast to Booker T. Washington's emphasis on industrial education).

Harriot Stanton Blatch, the daughter of Elizabeth Cady Stanton, formed the Equality League of Self-Supporting Women in New York in 1907, to work for suffrage and the right of women to combine marriage, motherhood, and paid labor.

The National Association for the Advancement of Colored People (NAACP) was founded in 1909. For the next two decades, it focused its protests and legislative activities primarily on anti-lynching campaigns, and female members formed a lobbying group called the Anti-Lynching Crusaders. The group succeeded in getting the Dyer Anti-Lynching bill out of a Congressional subcommittee (the first such success with anti-lynching legislation), and the bill passed the House of Representatives in 1922 but died in a Senate filibuster.

Angel Island, in San Francisco, a U.S. Immigration Station, served as the port of entry for Asian immigrants from 1910 to 1940.

Alice Paul organized the Congressional Committee within the languishing National American Woman Suffrage Association (NAWSA), and then in 1914 broke away to form the National Woman's Party (NWP). The new party introduced in 1923 an Equal Rights Amendment to the Constitution, a reflection of her focus on legal equality for women.

Carrie Chapman Catt emerged as a brilliant strategic organizer in campaigns from Idaho to New York between 1890 and 1915, and became NAWSA president in 1915. Her "Winning Plan," introduced in 1916, outlined a strategy to mobilize a disciplined army of suffragists from the ground up, campaigning in states where there was a chance of victory while simultaneously lobbying for passage of the Equal Rights Amendment.

Mary Church Terrell was an educator, civil rights leader, and first president of the National Association of Colored Women.

1913 Suffrage Parade was held in Washington, D.C., on March 3, by suffragists to demand an amendment to the Constitution forbidding the states from disfranchising citizens on account of gender.

Florence Kelley, a progressive suffragist and social reformer, contributed to the development of state and federal labor and social welfare legislation. She served as executive director of the National Consumer's League from 1899 to her death in 1932.

Jane Addams, founder in 1889 and director of Hull House, a Chicago welfare agency, was a progressive suffragist.

Locke, California, was an all-Chinese rural community built in 1913 on leased land because the California Asian Land Act forbade Asian Americans the right to own land.

Marcus Garvey, a Jamaican immigrant who after World War I founded the Universal Negro Improvement Association, the largest mass movement of African Americans until then, was the preeminent black nationalist and Pan-Africanist in American history.

Takao Ozawa v. United States resulted in a 1921 Supreme Court ruling that Japanese immigrants were ineligible for American citizenship.

United States v. Bhagat Singh Thind was a case in which the Supreme Court ruled in 1923 that Asian Indians were ineligible for U.S. citizenship. The case redefined whiteness, asserting that although historical and anthropological evidence suggested the Asian Indians were white, they were still not white because American society did not accept them as such.

Nixon v. Herndon was a 1927 U.S. Supreme Court ruling that a Texas law barring blacks from voting in the Democratic Party primary election was a violation of the Fourteenth Amendment.

Henry Gerber, a World War I veteran, founded the Chicago Society for Human Rights in 1924, the first gay rights group on record. He recruited members and published the newsletter, *Friendship and Freedom*, the first documented gay civil rights publication in the United States.

Charles Houston, academic dean of Howard University's Law School from 1929 to 1935, trained lawyers such as Thurgood Marshall, who later led the NAACP's legal campaigns for racial advancement.

Mary McLeod Bethune founded Daytona Normal and Industrial Institute for Negro Girls (now Bethune-Cookman College) in 1904 and was one of the first female leaders of a black institution of higher education. She was also the most prominent African American feminist leader of her times, an advisor to President Franklin D. Roosevelt on minority groups, and the director in charge of Negro Affairs in the New Deal National Youth Administration.

Eleanor Roosevelt, wife of President Franklin D. Roosevelt, was the most powerful female political activist of this era. Through her newspaper column and well-publicized travels, as well as her unofficial role as presidential advisor, she wielded enormous influence both in public and behind the scenes.

Missouri ex rel Gaines v. Canada was a 1938 suit that proved to be the most important desegregation case of this era. The Supreme Court determined that Missouri must provide a black student with the same education it provided to a white student.

Gibbs v. Board of Education was a case in which the Supreme Court in 1936 ordered the equalization of white and black teachers' salaries in Montgomery County, Maryland.

Bert Corona was a principal Chicano leader in the twentieth century. He founded or co-founded at least four important Chicano civil rights and advocacy organizations since the 1930s. No Chicano leader had a longer history of defending the rights of Chicano and Mexican immigrant workers.

Congress of Spanish Speaking People (El Congreso de Pueblos que Hablan Español) was formed in 1939. It was the first pan-Hispanic civil rights organization in the nation with a broad agenda for the protection of Mexican Americans, Mexican immigrants, and other Hispanic groups across the nation. Spearheaded by Luisa Moreno and a group of Los Angeles-based Hispanic leaders, the first Congress meeting represented more than 800,000 Hispanics from hundreds of local organizations and labor unions.

Suffragists picketing the White House, 1917
Photograph courtesy of the Library of Congress (LC-USZ62-31799 DLC)

PART 4. BIRTH OF THE CIVIL RIGHTS MOVEMENT, 1941-1954

World War II accelerated social change. Work in wartime industry and service in the armed forces, combined with the ideals of democracy, spawned a new civil rights agenda at home that forever transformed American life. Black migration to the North, where the right to vote was available, encouraged the Democratic and Republican Parties to solicit African American supporters. Changes in public policy at the federal level augured the end of racial segregation, and civil rights became a national issue for the first time since the Reconstruction era.

The armed forces blended soldiers and sailors from across the nation into military units, although minorities were confined to racially segregated commands or occupations. The defense industry created jobs that eventually brought about social and legislative reform. Employers encouraged millions of married women and mothers to work outside the home for the first time, a move that for some women led to postwar employment. Approximately 65,000 Indians left their reservations to work in the wartime industries and serve in the armed forces. African Americans threatened a "March on Washington" in 1941, in their demand for a fair share of jobs and an end to segregation in government departments and the armed forces. President Roosevelt responded by taking action to ban discrimination in defense industries. To assure compliance, he formed the Federal Employment Practices Committee (FEPC); its hearings exposed racial discrimination practices and helped migrants in the North get work. The formation of the FEPC also led to the first legal case centered on civil rights issues regarding equal employment for Hispanics, whose leaders appeared before the FEPC and protested the exclusion of Hispanics from many war industries because employers considered them "aliens" despite their American citizenship.

The war's Double V campaign (democracy abroad, democracy at home) also inspired gays and lesbians to civil rights activism when they encountered varying degrees of toleration and persecution in the armed forces. Although they were banned from military service, gays and lesbians enlisted or were conscripted anyway. Immediately after the war, gay and lesbian veterans briefly fought dishonorable discharges for sexual orientation, thereby setting the stage for the emerging homophile movement when in 1950 gays and lesbians asserted the right to gather in public places.

Even though minorities served in the military, those at home still faced racial discrimination from federal and local governments. Nearly 110,000 persons of Japanese descent from Oregon, Washington, and California were removed to internment camps pursuant to Executive Order 9066, which authorized the clearing of civilians from "military areas" but was only applied to Japanese Americans. In the Zoot Suit Riots of 1943, white servicemen in Los Angeles attacked Hispanic teenagers, who received no police protection. Chinese Americans, emboldened in part by the role of China as an American ally in the war, struggled against America's deeply rooted and institutionalized anti-Chinese racism, thereby inching closer to abolishing racist ideology in immigration policies. Six states denied American Indians access to the ballot, basing their decision on illiteracy, residency, nontaxation, and wardship status.

World War II spurred a new militancy among African Americans. The NAACP—emboldened by the record of black servicemen in the war, a new corps of brilliant young lawyers, and steady financial support from white philanthropists—initiated major attacks against discrimination and segregation, even in the Jim Crow South. Legal challenges to the *Plessy* doctrine dominated civil rights activities during the postwar era, culminating with the Supreme Court's 1954 decision in *Brown v. Board of Education*, which many scholars consider the birth of the modern civil rights movement.

Social pressure to end segregation also increased during and after the war. In 1944, the publication of Gunnar Myrdal's classic study of race relations, *An American Dilemma,* "offered an uncompromising account of the long history of racial injustice and a candid analysis of the economics of inequality."[4] President Harry S Truman continued President Roosevelt's use of executive powers outside of Congress to advance black civil rights. In 1946, Truman commissioned a study of racial inequities that called for an end to segregation in America. Completed in 1947, *To Secure These Rights* as well as legal victories in Supreme Court cases paved the way for the Second Reconstruction. In 1948, Truman issued Executive Order 9981, mandating "equality of treatment and opportunity for all those who serve in our country's defense . . . without regard to race, color, religion or national origin."

Examples of civil rights events and individuals

Repeal of Chinese Exclusion Acts came in 1943, authorizing a total of 105 Asian people to enter the country every year. Although the repeal was symbolic, it enabled Asian Americans and their allies later to challenge successfully anti-Asian racism in America's immigration laws.

Korematsu v. United States upheld the government's right to exclude people of Japanese ancestry from the West Coast based on military necessity. The Supreme Court handed down its bitterly contested decision in 1944.

Thurgood Marshall, head of the NAACP's Legal Defense and Educational Fund, led the legal fight that culminated in the *Brown v. Board of Education* decision.

Luisa Moreno and Josefina Fierro were the principal leaders of the Congress of Spanish Speaking People. Moreno was a Guatemalan immigrant who rose to the top leadership position in a Congress of Industrial Organizations union during the 1940s and was the main organizer of the first national meeting of the Congress. Fierro was the first national secretary of the Congress and later a member of the Sleepy Lagoon Defense Committee that helped overturn the mass conviction of Chicano youngsters in the infamous 1944 Sleepy Lagoon trial.

The Zoot Suit Riots were the first episodes of mass violence directed against Mexican Americans youths; they were targeted as un-American and deviant for wearing zoot suits. In 1943, white soldiers and sailors stationed around Los Angeles descended on downtown and East Los Angeles assaulting and terrorizing Mexican Americans for several months.

Smith v. Allright was a 1944 Supreme Court ruling that the Texas Democratic Party's use of the "white primary" to restrict black voting was unconstitutional under the Fifteenth Amendment.

---

[4] Eric Foner, *The Story of American Freedom* (New York: W. W. Norton & Company, 1998), 246.

The Mattachine Society was founded in 1950 by Communist Party member Harry Hay. The organization sponsored discussion groups, developed a theory of homosexuals as a cultural minority, fought police harassment, and founded the magazine, *One*, in 1953. An internal revolt in 1953 resulted in a new strategy of assimilation, but Mattachine continued to fight for basic civil rights. The society won a Supreme Court case it pursued after the Los Angeles postmaster refused to handle copies of *One* because he considered them obscene.

Stoumen v. Reilly was a 1951 California Supreme Court ruling found that it was not illegal for a public restaurant or bar to cater to homosexuals. Although it was still illegal under sodomy laws to engage in same-sex acts, the recognition of the right of public assembly for gay men and lesbians represented an important decision.

Brown v. Board of Education was the 1954 landmark Supreme Court decision that found racially segregated public schools unconstitutional and overturned the "separate but equal" doctrine in effect since 1896.

Monroe School, Brown v. Board of Education
National Historic Site
National Park Service photograph

PART 5. THE MODERN CIVIL RIGHTS MOVEMENT, 1954-1964

In the greatest mass movement in modern American history, black demonstrations swept the country seeking constitutional equality at the national level, as well as an end to Massive Resistance (state and local government-supported opposition to school desegregation) in the South. Presidential executive orders, the passage of two Civil Rights Acts, and the federal government's first military enforcement of civil rights brought an end to de jure segregation. The success of this movement inspired other minorities to employ similar tactics.

Three years after the Supreme Court ruled school segregation unconstitutional in *Brown v. Board of Education* and two years after the Montgomery, Alabama, bus boycott, President Dwight D. Eisenhower signed the first civil rights bill since Reconstruction. The 1957 Civil Rights Act created the independent U.S. Commission on Civil Rights. Although the Commission was limited to fact-finding, its reports helped shape the breakthrough Civil Rights Act of 1964, which also provided the Commission with greater authority.

Gains in civil rights varied for minorities during this era. Hispanics lost ground as they experienced mass deportations of legal and illegal immigrants in Operation Wetback, educational segregation in Southwest schools, and police brutality cases that rocked Los Angeles. In contrast, the re-emergence of a women's rights movement in the 1960s resulted in significant civil rights gains: adoption of the 1963 Equal Pay Act, the prohibition of inequality based on gender in the Civil Rights Act of 1964, and the breaching of barriers to employment for women.

Asian Americans likewise experienced gains and losses in civil rights. The McCarran-Walter Act of 1952 permitted Japanese immigrants to become citizens but contained restrictive quotas based on race and country of origin. Chinese Americans, especially during the McCarthy era, found themselves targets of suspicion and possible deportation following the Communist takeover of China. During this period, however, Asian Americans began their own social, cultural, and political initiatives to challenge the status quo and advance their civil rights.

During this time, the homophile movement grew and changed direction. Gays and lesbians in the "bar culture" engaged in various forms of resistance to police repression by insisting on their right to gather in public. In cities across the country, for example, working-class lesbian bars nurtured a world where women made public their same-sex desire. This cultural resistance, along with the formal political efforts of homophile organizations, laid the basis for the contemporary gay and lesbian movement.

African American mass demonstrations, televised racial violence, and the federally enforced desegregation of higher education institutions, as well as the black passive resistance movement of the early 1960s led to adoption of the landmark Civil Rights Act of 1964. Considered the most comprehensive civil rights legislation in U.S. history, the act granted the federal government strong enforcement powers in the area of civil rights. It prohibited tactics to limit voting; guaranteed racial and religious minorities equal access to public accommodations; outlawed job discrimination on the basis of race, color, religion, sex, or national origin; continued the U.S. Commission on Civil Rights; and established the Equal Employment Opportunity Commission.

Examples of civil rights events and individuals

Daughters of Bilitis (DOB) emerged in San Francisco in 1955 as the first national lesbian organization. Through its publication, the *Ladder*, DOB worked to prove the respectability of lesbians and to win acceptance within mainstream society.

Montgomery Bus Boycott occurred after Rosa Parks was arrested on December 1, 1955, for refusing to surrender her seat on a city bus to a white rider, as required by municipal law. The yearlong bus boycott that followed marked a new era in the modern civil rights movement.

Sit-in (nonviolent) movement began with the peaceful occupation of lunch counters on February 1, 1960, in Greensboro, North Carolina, as college students started a direct, but passive, assault on the denial of their rights to public facilities. The addition of young adults to the movement swelled the ranks of those participating in demonstrations.

Ella Baker was a black activist who in 1960 helped organize the Student Non-Violent Coordinating Committee, a decentralized group favoring grassroots politics to empower ordinary people to speak out.

Martin Luther King, Jr., was the preeminent African American leader of the civil rights movement. His unmatched eloquence, his strategy of nonviolent resistance, and his dignified and calm demeanor also inspired large numbers of whites to support the movement's goals. King rose to national notice with his leadership role in the Montgomery, Alabama, bus boycott of 1955-1956. The next year, elected head of the Southern Christian Leadership Conference, he adapted the nonviolent civil disobedience tactics of Gandhi to the civil rights movement. From then until his death, he was at the forefront of the movement. King was assassinated in Memphis, Tennessee, on April 4, 1968.

The March on Washington for civil rights and full employment in 1963 was the largest protest for African American rights at that time. It cemented the reputation of Martin Luther King, Jr., as the century's major national African American leader. On the steps of the Lincoln Memorial, on August 28, King gave his famous "I Have a Dream" oration.

1963 "March on Washington for
Jobs and Freedom"
Photograph by Abbie Rowe
National Park Service

Betty Friedan was the author of *The Feminine Mystique* (1963) and founder of the National Organization for Women who was devoted to obtaining full equality for women in public life. Her work and writings had a major influence on the prohibition of inequality based on gender in the Civil Rights Act of 1964. It resulted in creation of the Equal Employment Opportunity Commission and broke down barriers to employment for women.

Publication of *Drum*, the pioneering journal of the Janus Society of Philadelphia, launched in 1964 under its president Clark Polak. *Drum* was advertised as a place for "news for 'queers'," and "fiction for 'perverts'." *Drum* quickly outgrew all other homophile publications, gaining a circulation of 15,000.

President Lyndon B. Johnson signs the 1964 Civil Rights Act in the East Room of the White House as Martin Luther King, Jr. and others look on
Photograph by Cecil Stoughton, courtesy of the Lyndon Baines Johnson Library and Museum, National Archives and Record Administration

PART 6. THE SECOND REVOLUTION, 1964-1976

With the passage of the Civil Rights Act of 1964, the U.S. Commission on Civil Rights struggled with an agenda rapidly expanding in scope, complexity, and controversy. The Commission's work took on a national rather than a regional focus and concentrated on affirmative action and federal enforcement efforts. As impressive gains were made in African American civil rights, the Commission addressed claims from an expanding array of newly mobilized social movements and civil rights constituencies for similar protections and remedies.[5]

The Civil Rights Act made the enforcement of school desegregation possible. Faced with the prospect of losing federal funding, school boards and local governments produced plans to integrate schools. Late in the 1960s and early in the 1970s, the Commission investigated African American education as well as the educational isolation of Hispanic schoolchildren, a legacy of segregation dating from the turn of the century, and recommended changes.

The act's equal employment and other economic-opportunity features significantly affected minorities and women. For example, the Mexican farm workers' fight for economic justice and the Chicano Movement for dignity and identity became inexorably linked. The concept and practice of "affirmative action" significantly expanded the black middle class, although success was limited in breaking through "glass ceilings" in corporate ownerships and upper-management positions. In addition, the recurring "backlash" against affirmative action continued to leave most African Americans in a marginal economic position. Members of the Equal Employment Opportunity Commission (EEOC) urged the formation of a "civil rights lobby" for women analogous to the NAACP for African Americans to implement the act. The National Organization for Women (NOW) was founded, and women active in the civil rights, antiwar, and students' movements also began to raise the issue of women's equality. In government, executive branch remedies for past discrimination included developing a federal contract workforce reflecting the minority and gender makeup of the labor pool.

Even with the passage of the Civil Rights Act, minorities continued to face voting restrictions. The Supreme Court had made it clear, at least since 1944, that the Fifteenth Amendment granting citizens voting rights could not be denied or abridged. Yet, it took another twenty years and the Voting Rights Act of 1965 to provide the enforcement measures needed to protect African Americans and other minorities. The results were felt most significantly in the nation's urban areas, as well as in the Deep South where voter registration soared and black municipal officials were elected in large numbers. Many blacks gained control of local governments and paved the way for expanded political influence. Similar results were achieved in the Chicano Civil Rights Movement of 1965-1975. Throughout the twentieth century, various Hispanic advocacy organizations had openly protested against poll taxes and other tactics that kept Hispanics from registering to vote. Voting rights cases from the 1970s through the 1990s resulted in the election of Hispanics to previously all-white municipal and county councils and boards.

Late in the 1960s, the Black Power Movement advocated black pride, control over black institutions, and self-determination over integration. It began to replace the earlier strategy of nonviolent civil disobedience with a more militant and aggressive approach.

---

[5] Hugh Davis Graham, "The Civil Rights Commission: The First 40 Years," *Civil Rights Journal* (Fall 1997): 7.

Asian Americans continued to advance their civil rights issues. Many Filipino farm workers partnered with César Chávez and the United Farmworkers Union. Chinese, Filipino, and Japanese students at San Francisco State University united in 1968 to call for ethnic studies programs, a movement shared with African Americans, Hispanics, and American Indians. The burgeoning war in Vietnam eventually resulted in large-scale emigration from Southeast Asia to America, and Congress passed legislation to assist the new immigrants.

Homophile groups throughout the country also became more militant, speaking out against police entrapment, working to educate the public and professionals about homosexuality, and fighting against discrimination in government employment, to counter the earlier McCarthyite linking of Communist subversion and homosexuality. The Stonewall riot during a June 1969 police raid on the Stonewall Inn in Greenwich Village traditionally marks the beginning of the Gay Liberation Movement, although the emergence was in fact more gradual and more complex. In the aftermath of the riot, gay liberation fronts spread like wildfire from New York to other major cities, as well as to college campuses across the country. Women broke away from male-dominated organizations to form lesbian feminist groups and collectives. The struggle shifted from the right to public space to education, including the demand for gay and lesbian studies in universities; legal protection for gay, lesbian, bisexual (and, eventually, transgender) people; and equal employment, including in the schools, the military, and government. The modern gay, lesbian, bisexual, and transgender movement emerged from this period of activism. In 1974, the first federal civil rights bill for gay men and lesbians was introduced in Congress.

The last of the great civil rights statutes of the 1960s was the Fair Housing Act of 1968, which banned racial discrimination in the sale and rental of housing throughout the nation. The emergence of modern suburbia in the mid-twentieth century included rigid racial covenants that left a legacy and reinforced racial barriers to public education and jobs. Private developers refused to allow minorities to rent or own homes and federal agencies insured mortgages with racially restricted provisions, all in support of the whites' fears that integration would lower their property values and quality of life. The Fair Housing Act helped shift the center of the civil rights movement from the rural South to the urban North, where racial concentration in housing was more prevalent. The shift spawned a campaign for residential integration and equal housing there and across the nation.

Examples of civil rights events, places, and individuals

Selma-to-Montgomery march, in Alabama, was led by Martin Luther King, Jr., and others for voting rights. After a vicious attack by state and local police officers, demonstrators under federal protection marched from Selma to the state capitol in Montgomery, Alabama. The march, with its "Bloody Sunday" in March 7, 1965, led to the landmark Voting Rights Act of that year.

The Edmund Pettus Bridge, Selma, Alabama, along the Selma to Montgomery National Historic Trail
Photograph courtesy of the Alabama Historical Society

Homophile militant protests were launched in 1965. They included picket lines at the Civil Service Commission building, the State Department, the Pentagon, the White House, and in Philadelphia on the Fourth of July, at Independence Hall. In Washington, contingents of women and men carried signs proclaiming "Homosexuals Should be Judged as Individuals" and "Support Homosexual Rights." In "annual reminders" from 1966 to 1969, protesters at Independence Hall reminded onlookers that the Declaration of Independence had not brought freedom to all.

The Immigration and Nationality Act was passed in 1965. It abolished the racist "national origin" basis for allocating annual immigration quota for individual countries. Asian nations received the same quota as European countries.

Aileen Hernandez was the only woman member of the first Equal Employment Opportunity Commission. When Title VII (prohibiting employment discrimination) was not implemented, Hernandez urged the formation of a civil rights lobby for women analogous to the NAACP.

Malcolm X was a charismatic and controversial African American leader who came to symbolize the Black Power Movement. While in prison in 1952, he became a convert to Elijah Muhammad's Nation of Islam. He later renounced it and became a traditional Muslim in 1964. His views on racial cooperation and black nationalism also evolved to the point of engagement with the non-violent civil rights movement. He was assassinated in New York City on February 21, 1965.

Black Panther Party was one of the militant black groups that emerged during the Black Power period following the passage of major civil rights legislation.

Ethnic studies were advocated in 1968 by Asian American students at San Francisco State University as serious topics for research and teaching. Widely accepted today, the concept was considered radical at that time.

The Stonewall riot occurred on the night of June 27, 1969, when police raided the Stonewall Inn in Greenwich Village. What had happened so many times before in so many other places this time provoked prolonged resistance. Fighting back and sparking a night of rioting, the patrons of the Stonewall Inn came to stand for militant resistance and gay pride.

César Chávez and United Farm Workers (UFW) Union Headquarters (known as the Forty Acres) in Delano, California, are symbolic of the Chicano civil rights movement in the second half of the 1960s. Although Chávez remained a labor leader, his practices of nonviolent civil disobedience and his struggle for the rights of ordinary workers now place him in the pantheon of great civil rights leaders in U.S. history.

East Los Angeles Blowouts occurred in 1968 when more than a thousand Chicano high school students on the east side of Los Angeles walked out of their classes to protest inferior educational opportunities and discrimination. This event sparked reform for Chicano students in segregated schools.

First National Chicano Youth Liberation Conference was sponsored in Denver in 1969 by Corky Gonzales' Crusade for Justice to assemble Chicano youth from throughout the nation to declare their rights and to promote an ethnic nationalist movement. Much of the symbolism and rhetoric of the Chicano Student Movement emanates from this meeting.

La Raza Unida Party symbolized the political aspirations of Chicano youth. The organizational convention of this first and only Chicano political party met with 3,000 delegates in El Paso, Texas, in 1972. Jose Angel Gutierrez was elected as chairman, but his election divided the party between Gutierrez and supporters of Corky Gonzales. The party had early successes in Texas communities but soon collapsed.

Mexican American Legal Defense and Education Fund (MALDEF) was founded in 1968. It became the primary voting rights and civil rights advocacy organization for Mexican Americans. Headquartered first in San Antonio and then later moved to San Francisco and, finally, to Los Angeles, MALDEF won several important voting rights cases over the years.

The Philadelphia Plan was the creation of President Richard M. Nixon's administration in 1969, requiring contractors bidding on federal and federally assisted construction projects to hire a fixed number of minority group members. The measure was first applied in Philadelphia. In 1971, the U.S. Court of Appeals for the Third Circuit upheld the plan's legality.

Formation of the National Gay Task Force took place in 1973, when a group of mostly white middle-class gay men interested in political action formed it (later renamed the National Gay and Lesbian Task Force). The group focused on national issues and sought to bring gay liberation into the mainstream of American civil rights.

The Indochina Migration and Refugee Assistance Act was passed in 1975 to aid residents of Vietnam, Cambodia, and Laos who fled for their lives once the United States withdrew from Vietnam. More than 130,000 refugees came to the United States, marking the beginning of large-scale South and East Asian immigration to the United States. This law reversed years of immigration policies that sought to severely limit or exclude Asian groups from immigrating to the United States and becoming citizens and signaled greater acceptance of Asians as an integral part of American society.

PART 7. THE AMERICAN INDIAN MOVEMENT

The chronology of the American Indian Movement is treated separately in this framework because the nature of the interactions between American Indians and the United States is substantially different than that of other minority groups. Tens of thousands of American Indians suffered from colonial and national expansion and gave their lives in defense of their people and their country. The federal government treated Indians variously as independent nations, dependent peoples, and obstacles to be removed from the path of progress, sometimes by separate confinement on reservations and other times by forced assimilation. Unlike other minority groups, American Indians have fought wars and negotiated treaties with the United States, which singled them out for special consideration in the Constitution. They have struggled not only for civil rights in the conventional sense, but also for their autonomy, language, culture, religion, and land. Their story is unlike that of any other nonwhite group in the United States.

Before the coming of European colonial powers to the shores of North America and the founding of the United States, hundreds of American Indian cultures thrived here. Religious beliefs, worldviews, cosmologies, and environmental surroundings shaped the structure of their governments, institutions, economies, and material culture. There was, and continues to be, a great deal of diversity among American Indian populations, languages, and cultures.

The European and then the dominant white American society viewed Indians as the "Other": warlike barriers to expansion or "noble savages." What to do with Indians became a national dilemma that boiled down to two options: assimilate or perish.

Following the English model of colonialism, the federal government viewed Indian tribes as separate nations and treated them differently from white Americans. The U.S. Constitution contains two references to Indians. First, Congress has the power to regulate trade among the various states, foreign nations, and Indian nations. Second, the executive branch has the responsibility of negotiating treaties with foreign powers, including with Indian nations, as well as a military relationship as commander-in-chief. The judicial branch has the duty to interpret the Constitution. Federal policy has largely been based on these constitutional directives.

For the purposes of this framework, Indian-United States government relations have been divided into the following five policy eras, with land issues central to the development of this relationship.

TREATY-MAKING ERA, 1776-1871

Colonial and then American expansion into Indian country sparked a series of bloody engagements that continued until the 1890s. Throughout this era, the federal government and Indian nations negotiated hundreds of treaties stipulating that the government would provide the Indians with educational, medical, and housing services. The Supreme Court rendered decisions that defined the legal and political status of Indian nations, usually in ways that restricted Indian sovereignty. Congress also enacted numerous laws pertaining specifically to American Indians. In 1830, Congress passed and President Andrew Jackson signed the Indian Removal Act, and many American Indians were forcibly removed from their ancestral homes and pushed west across the Mississippi River, while western settlers appropriated Indian lands, thereby destroying Native cultural and political autonomy. Out of this history emerged what is called the trust doctrine.

The defining moment of this doctrine came in 1831, when Chief Justice John Marshall described the Cherokee nation as being "in a state of pupilage," resembling that of "a ward to his guardian."[6] The following year, he pictured the Cherokee Nation as a "domestic nation," and that a "weak state, in order to provide for its safety, may place itself under the protection of one more powerful without stripping itself of the right of government and ceasing to be a state."[7] Thus, the federal government assumed extensive powers over Indians, although the motive was mostly to open Indian lands for non-Indian settlement.

Examples of civil rights individuals, places, and events

Tecumseh, a Shawnee, organized a confederacy of tribes in the Ohio Valley soon after 1810 to preserve Indian lands and cultures. In 1813, Tecumseh was killed at the Battle of the Thames, effectively ending collective military Indian resistance east of the Mississippi River. Tecumseh was probably the earliest pan-Indian leader in U.S. history.

Prophetstown was an Indiana community founded by Tecumseh and his brother Tenskwatawa, also called The Prophet. Their followers gathered there to defend their lands and ways of life from the United States. In 1811, a militia army destroyed the camp.

Indian resistance, under the leadership of Black Hawk, Crazy Horse, Cochise, and other Indian leaders increased during this period as Indians struggled to maintain their lands and cultures against the U.S. military effort to displace them.

John Marshall was the third chief justice of the U.S. Supreme Court. His Court made important decisions in Indian rights, especially during the years of Indian removal of the 1830s that defined rights of territoriality and relationships between Indian tribes and federal and state governments.

John Ross, chief of the Cherokee nation, protested the removal of his people from their ancestral lands and in 1838 led his people into forced exile from east of the Mississippi.

ASSIMILATION AND ALLOTMENT ERA, 1871-1934

Devastated by disease, economic deprivation, and military struggles, most Indians had been confined to reservations by the 1870s. This era was characterized by federal attempts to turn Indians into mirror images of white Americans through the allotment of tribal landholdings to individuals, education, and other means to eradicate the Indians' culture and spirit.

In the Indian Appropriations Act of 1871, Congress took away sovereign nation status from tribes without awarding them U.S. citizenship. They were therefore subject to the law but not protected by the rights of citizenship. Alarmed Indian reformers called for citizenship through

---

[6] *Cherokee Nation v. State of Georgia*, 30 U.S. 1 (1831).
[7] *Worcester v. Georgia*, 31 U.S. 515 (1832).

the allotment, or redistribution of reservation land in small parcels, to individual tribal members. Thereafter, Congress passed the Dawes Act of 1887, also known as the General Allotment Act. The act offered Native Americans individual land ownership and full citizenship. Under this process, Congress envisioned individuals with more control over land until tribes no longer existed. Tribal land not parceled out to individual Indians changed hands from Indians to whites and ultimately opened up more than 100 million acres to white development.[8] Over the next three decades, the Dawes Act awarded citizenship to thousands of American Indians. In addition, American Indian veterans of World War I received citizenship status. Eventually, all Native Americans gained citizenship under the Snyder Act of 1924. Federal policy, however, treated them as wards of the U.S. government and curtailed their full citizenship rights. They were denied the right to travel freely, manage their own money, vote (in some states), and purchase firearms and alcohol.

Examples of civil rights events and individuals

Geronimo, a Chiricahua Apache military leader in Arizona, led the Apaches in defense of their way of life beginning in the 1870s. Finally coming to terms with General Nelson A. Miles in 1886, he and his small band of followers were shipped in exile to Florida, Alabama, and Oklahoma. He never returned to his beloved Arizona but died a prisoner of war in 1909 at Fort Sill, Oklahoma.

Lone Wolf v. Hitchcock was a 1903 U.S. Supreme Court case in which Lone Wolf, a Kiowa leader, sued Ethan Hitchcock, the Secretary of the Interior, to block the allotment of reservation lands. The Court ruled that Congress had plenary power over Indian nations, was therefore virtually exempt from judicial oversight.

Wassaja (Carlos Montezuma) was captured as a boy and educated in the dominant white society. Wassaja became a physician in Chicago, but not forgetting his roots, he headed a successful drive during the 1910s to prevent the federal government from removing his Yavapai relatives from the Fort McDowell Reservation to a less desirable location.

Allotment process resistance was led by individuals such as Redbird Smith (Cherokee) and Chitto Harjo (Muskogee) early in the 1900s against the allotment process.

The Indian Citizenship Act of 1924, also known as the Snyder Act, was passed by Congress to award citizenship to all Indians born in the United States.

INDIAN NEW DEAL ERA, 1934-1945

In 1926, the Secretary of the Interior commissioned the Institute for Government Research (Brookings Institution in 1927) to survey the economic and social conditions of the American Indians. Issued in 1928 and named for the survey director, Lewis Meriam, the scathing report declared assimilation a disastrous failure. In response, the federal government next embarked on a policy called the Indian New Deal. Rather than trying to assimilate Indians, it supported many functions of Indian government in the "desire to restore Indian culture and heritage, address

---

[8] James S. Olson, ed., *Encyclopedia of American Indian Civil Rights* (Westport, CT: Greenwood Press, 1997), 6-7.

communal land base and land purchase issues, and regenerate tribal self-government."[9] The Indian New Deal used various New Deal agency programs such as the Public Works Administration to meet these goals.

Drawing heavily on the Meriam Report, Congress adopted a major reform measure. The Indian Reorganization Act of 1934 canceled the general allotment policy and changed the Bureau of Indian Affairs (BIA) procedures regarding economic development and community self-government. The act authorized tribes to adopt their own constitutions and bylaws. However, many tribes were not prepared for self-government and no major transfers of governmental functions from the BIA to the tribes occurred.[10]

Examples of civil rights events

The Indian Reorganization Act of 1934 repudiated the 1887 Dawes Act and attempted to secure new rights for Indians on reservations. Written by the Commissioner of Indian Affairs John Collier, this law ended the land allotment program under the Dawes Act, provided funding for Indians to purchase land, returned local self government on a tribal basis, and promoted the preservation of Indian culture.

Oklahoma Indian Welfare Act was passed in 1936 and extended the Indian Reorganization Act's provisions to include Oklahoma Indians.

National Congress of American Indians fought for Indian sovereignty and political and treaty rights between 1941 and 1954.

TERMINATION ERA, 1945-1960[11]

After World War II, the pendulum of federal policy swung back to absorbing Indians into mainstream society by terminating the trust relationship, relocating or assimilating Indian people, and compensating Indian tribes illegitimately seized lands. Congress sought to end the federal relationship and turn Indian affairs over to the states. During the 1950s, more than a hundred nations were terminated, leaving them susceptible to land loss and poverty. Tribal leaders resisted termination, preferring the trust relationship with the federal government over the lack of

---

[9] University Publications of America, "Native Americans and the New Deal: The Office Files of John Collier, 1933-1945," 1995, 1, www.lexisnexis.com/academic/guides/native_american/collier htm.

[10] Donald L. Burnett, Jr., "An Historical Analysis of the 1968 'Indian Civil Rights' Act," in *Civil Rights in American History: Major Historical Interpretations* (New York: Garland Publishing Inc., 1987), 198–199.

[11] Not all sources agree on the dates (and names) of chronological eras of American Indian history. For the termination era, this framework uses the 1945 beginning date based on the shift in policy following World War II, and uses the 1960 ending date as the one most secondary sources provided. See Kermit L. Hall, ed. in chief, *The Oxford Companion to the Supreme Court* (New York: Oxford University Press, 1992), 579; American Indian Civics Project, "American Indian Issues: An Introductory and Curricular Guide for Educators," http://www humboldt.edu/~go1kellogg/Chrono.html; James S. Olson, ed., *Encyclopedia of American Indian Civil Rights* (Westwood, CT: Greenwood Press, 1997); George Pierre Castile, *To Show Heart: Native American Self-Determination and Federal Indian Policy, 1960-1975* (Tucson: University of Arizona Press, 1998); and Samuel R. Cook, "What is Indian Self-Determination," *Red Ink*, vol. 3, no. 1 (1 May 1994), http://faculty.smu.edu/twalker/ samrcook htm. (This last journal is a Native American student publication of the University of Arizona's American Indian Graduate Center.)

support at the state and local levels for Indian interests. American Indian voting rights also came to the fore before the U.S. Supreme Court during this period.

Examples of civil rights events, places, and individuals

The Indian Claims Commission Act was passed by Congress in 1946 and created a commission, that proved controversial, to review claims by various tribes against the U.S. government for land seizures and to implement compensation.

Relocation programs through the BIA provided job training and funds to move Indians from reservations to large cities, but assimilation failed once again as many American Indians rejected city life.

Harrison v. Laveen was a 1948 U.S. Supreme Court decision that found Arizona's restrictions on Indian voting rights unconstitutional.

Allen v. Merrell was a 1956 Supreme Court decision that overturned a Utah court ruling denying the franchise to Indians for fear that they might gain control of the county government.

SELF-DETERMINATION ERA, 1960-1975[12]

During the termination era, Indians had lost much of their remaining land, religious freedom, and traditional modes of economic production. The federal government had committed itself to provide certain services in return for the land, but Indians still faced numerous injustices. The Indian civil rights movement began in the 1960s as activists sought self-determination, land restoration, and traditional hunting and fishing privileges. By the mid-1960s, the term "Red Power" described the movement as one inspired by the "Black Power" movement of African Americans. American Indian activists targeted the federal government with protests, demanding legislation to correct the situation. They sought recognition of treaty rights and the restoration of tribal sovereignty. Over the objections of Indian governments, however, Congress passed the Indian Civil Rights Act of 1968. This law imposed portions of the federal Bill of Rights on Indian governments, thus limiting tribal sovereignty and representing federal government intrusion into tribes' internal affairs. The founding of the American Indian Movement (AIM), demonstrations, marches, and the occupation of high-profile sites characterize this period.

---

[12] Secondary sources cite this era as ending in either the 1970s or the 1990s. This framework uses the 1975 ending date based on the emergence of a "Self-Governance" era that begins in either 1975 or 1979. See American Indian Civics Project, "American Indian Issues." Harvard University's Government Innovators Network website "Trust Resource Management" states how the Indian Self-Determination and Education Assistance Act of 1975 ushered in a new era of self-governance, http://www.innovations.harvard.edu/awards.html?id=6173. Joshua P. Fershee of the University of North Dakota – School of Law proposed a new concept of Self-Domination to replace and move beyond the Self-Determination era in "From Self-Determination to Self-Domination: Native Americans, Western Culture, and the Promise of Constitutional-Based Reform," *Valapraiso University Law Review,* vol. 39, no. 1, 2004: 1-26.

Examples of civil rights events, places, and individuals

Juan de Jesús Romero witnessed the involuntary transfer of thousands of acres of Taos land to the Carson National Forest, including Blue Lake, when a small boy in 1906 at Taos Pueblo in northern New Mexico. In Taos beliefs, the Creator had given them Blue Lake. Before long, non-Indian encroachments into the surrounding area disrupted many of the shrines. Facing this threat to their spiritual well being, the Taos people demanded the return of their sacred land. After Romero became the cacique (a religious leader) of his people, he led the struggle for the return of Blue Lake. In 1970, then in his nineties, Romero witnessed President Richard M. Nixon sign a bill that returned Blue Lake and 25,000 acres.

Fish-ins were held in the 1960s by American Indians in the Pacific Northwest in support of their treaty rights. Beginning with *Sohappy v. Washington State* (1968), David Sohappy, Sr., sued for fishing and other treaty rights. In *United States v. Washington* (1974), a federal district court held that many western Washington Indian nations had a right to half of the salmon catch.[13]

National Indian Education Association was established in 1969 to give American Indians and Alaska Natives a national voice in their struggle to obtain educational equality.

Indian Education: A National Tragedy—A National Challenge was the 1969 report of the Senate Committee on Labor and Public Welfare that exposed many shortcomings in the education of Indian children and offered recommendations for change.

Formation of local Indian school boards resulted from a 1969 shift in BIA policy that encouraged the formation of such boards. The new policy also offered Indian governments an opportunity to assume management of schools administered by the BIA.

American Indian Movement (AIM) was organized in 1968 in Minneapolis, Minnesota, in response to police brutality. AIM soon began to speak out for Indian sovereignty, religious freedom, treaty rights, and cultural survival. Significant individuals include Vernon Bellecourt, Russell Means, Clyde Bellecourt, and Dennis Banks.

Maria Pearson, a Sioux, in 1972 led the opposition in Iowa to a discriminatory state law that required the immediate reburial of non-Indian remains and the curation of Indian remains in a state facility for study in perpetuity. Her action contributed to the rise of the repatriation movement that sought to end the abuses committed against American Indian remains.

Robert E. Lewis, governor of Zuni Pueblo in New Mexico, began a "home rule" experiment in 1970. By the end of the following year, Zuni Pueblo had taken over control of its own affairs from the BIA. Other Indian nations followed suit.

Annie Wauneka, tribal leader of the Navajo Nation and public health activist, devoted her life to improving health conditions on the Navajo reservation. During her three terms on the Tribal Council, she promoted the benefits of modern medicine in her travels throughout the reservation

---

[13] The case is known as the *Boldt Decision* after the presiding judge, George Boldt.

and on weekly radio broadcasts. In particular, she is recognized for her contributions to defeating tuberculosis among the Navajo beginning in the 1950s.

Hank Adams, an Assinboine-Sioux Indian, worked for the National Indian Youth Council and the National Congress of American Indians, and in 1968 became national director of the Survival of American Indians Association, a group dedicated to Native American fishing rights. Adams led the struggle against oppressive state laws that denied Washington Indians their treaty rights to fish in the usual and customary places.

Anna Mae Aquash, a Micmac Indian, was an AIM activist who participated in the 1973 Wounded Knee occupation. Murdered in 1975 on the Pine Ridge Reservation in South Dakota, she became a symbol of the Indian rights movement.

Ada Deer, a member of the Menominee tribe and a nationally noted activist, played a leading role during the 1970s towards successfully restoring the Menominee Indians to a federally recognized nation. Efforts made by Deer and others brought national attention to the issue of termination. In 1993, Deer became head of the BIA.

Bureau of Indian Affairs headquarters was taken over in November 1972 by members of AIM while on its Trail of Broken Treaties, a caravan traveling from the West Coast to Washington, D.C., to garner media support for self-determination. While demonstrating at the BIA building, violence broke out and the Native Americans occupied the building. After six days, the government agreed to consider AIM's demands for reform, but eventually rejected most of them, leading pan-Indian activists to renew violent protests against federal Indian policy.

Tribally controlled higher education began in 1971 at Tsaili on the Navajo reservation, when Diné College (first established as Navajo Community College in 1968) became the first tribally controlled college in the United States. Deganawida-Quetzelcoatl University was established in Davis, California, at about the same time. Within the next decade another two dozen such institutions were founded in Indian country.

Alcatraz Island, a former federal prison located in San Francisco Bay, was occupied by American Indian activists from 1969 to 1971, a pivotal event in Indian political history that awakened the consciousness of Indians concerning land, education, sovereignty, and poverty issues. Activists wanted to use the island for an educational and cultural center and to publicize the mistreatment of Indian peoples.

Alcatraz Island,
Golden Gate National Recreation Area
National Park Service photograph

THEMATIC FRAMEWORK

Theme studies are an effective way of assessing whether or not places are nationally significant in American history. They provide a historic context within which to evaluate properties, establish registration guidelines, and identify places that should be studied for national designation. A thematic framework for civil rights history should be based on the voting rights, public accommodations, equal employment, and equal education provisions of the great civil rights acts of the 1960s. These acts include the Civil Rights Act of 1964, the Voting Rights Act of 1965, and the Fair Housing Act of 1968. Other prominent themes identified in this study's overview include criminal injustice, immigrant rights, and American Indian civil rights. These themes are characterized below.

A major question in developing a framework for identifying civil rights sites is to what degree the National Park Service has already identified and interpreted civil rights-related events, persons, and places. Thus, each theme description also summarizes whether the National Park Service has conducted any surveys or designated National Historic Landmarks and whether Congress established any National Park System units within the respective context. Civil rights-related National Historic Landmarks and National Park System units are listed in Table 1 of this study.

THEMES

- **Equal Education** – The legal fight for equal education led the way toward overturning state- and federally-sponsored segregation. From the U.S. Supreme Court's decisions in *Plessy* in 1896 to *Brown v. Board of Education* in 1954, court-ordered school desegregation unlocked the nation's potential to achieve equality as the Constitution mandates. After almost a decade of massive resistance to school desegregation, the Civil Rights Act of 1964 authorized the Justice Department to sue education systems that continued to discriminate. Minority-led legal challenges to and nonviolent protests of segregated public education and federal enforcement of court-ordered desegregation characterize this theme.

  The story of school desegregation is told in the National Historic Landmarks theme study, *Racial Desegregation in Public Education in the United States* (2000). Authorized by the Little Rock Central High School National Historic Site enabling legislation, the theme study contains a comprehensive history of the Asian American, Hispanic, African American, and Native American (including Alaska Natives and Native Hawaiians) school segregation and desegregation experiences. As a result of this study, sites exceptional for illustrating educational equality between 1849 and 1967, such as Howard High School in Wilmington, Delaware, have received National Historic Landmark designation. Also, National Park Service units, like the Brown v. Board of Education National Historic Site in Topeka, Kansas, tell the story of school segregation and the enforcement of court-ordered desegregation.

- **Public Accommodation** – Minority groups, Congress, and the Supreme Court have debated and interpreted the right to public accommodations for more than one hundred years. The nonviolent boycotts and sit-in campaigns staged by activists in the 1940s and 1950s intensified in the 1960s as the media exposed violent segregationists' reactions to the nation and the world. The Civil Rights Act of 1964 banned racial discrimination in public accommodations.

National Historic Landmarks depict certain watershed events in the African American struggle for integrated public accommodations. At Constitution Hall in Washington, D.C., the Daughters of the American Revolution denied access in 1939 to singer Marian Anderson. Dexter Avenue Baptist Church in Montgomery, Alabama, depicts the grassroots effort to boycott Montgomery city buses in 1955-56 following Rosa Parks's refusal to yield her seat on a city bus to a white man. Stonewall Inn symbolizes the 1969 gay and lesbian riots for the right to gather in public places.

The civil rights overview identifies other places, individuals, organizations, and events associated with fighting discrimination in public accommodations. The 1960s sit-in movement began at the Woolworth lunch counter in Greensboro, North Carolina. The 1963 march in Birmingham, Alabama, exposed racial violence to the American public. Ella Baker, a founder of the Student Nonviolent Coordinating Committee, helped organize sit-in movements. Many places associated with this theme have been identified in the draft National Historic Landmarks theme study *Civil Rights in America: Racial Desegregation of Public Accommodations*.

- **Voting** – Acquiring access to the ballot was a milestone in the path to full civil rights for minorities and women. Securing the franchise represents political freedom, the right to self-government, and the transformation of the nature of American politics. The franchise was extended to all male citizens in 1870 and to women in 1920. The Civil Rights Acts of 1957 and 1964 respectively strengthened federal authority and expanded federal guarantees of civil rights in voting. Despite these guarantees, state and local governments used gerrymandering and literacy tests to defeat and discourage minority voting. Only the Voting Rights Act of 1965 breached the last barriers to voting. Its provisions extended to American Indians, Hispanic Americans, Asian Americans, and other minorities. Violence, mass demonstrations, and coalescing minority groups characterize the voting rights story.

  The National Park Service tells much of the voting rights story in its National Historic Landmarks and National Park System units. For example, the Women's Rights National Historical Park in Seneca Falls, New York preserves and interprets the history of the early woman's rights movement. The park includes the Elizabeth Cady Stanton home and the Wesleyan Chapel, site of the first Women's Rights Convention in 1848. Other units and National Historic Landmarks recognize meeting places and homes of influential women suffragists and African American women's organizations. African American-related sites include abolitionists' homes, grassroots meeting places, and the 1965 Selma to Montgomery marching route. The National Park Service has completed the draft National Historic Landmarks theme study *Civil Rights in America: Racial Voting Rights* that identifies other places to study for National Historic Landmark consideration.

- **Housing** – Supported by both private developers and by federal policy, racially restrictive housing policies and covenants institutionalized residential segregation for all minorities until

33

1948, when the Supreme Court found racially restrictive housing covenants unconstitutional. This decision eventually led to substantial changes in housing patterns throughout the country. Even so, restrictive covenants remained in effect until Congress adopted the Fair Housing Act of 1968. This act marked a transition in the civil rights movement as enforcement efforts shifted from the rural South, where the Civil Rights Act of 1964 had gained African Americans access to public accommodations and employment opportunities, to the urban North where racial minorities faced housing discrimination.

One National Historic Landmark is associated with the housing theme. The Shelley House in St. Louis, Missouri, is the home of the plaintiffs in *Shelley v. Kramer* (1948) in which the U.S. Supreme Court ruled that racially restrictive housing covenants violated the Fourteenth Amendment. The National Park Service is preparing a theme study entitled *Civil Rights in America: Racial Discrimination in Housing*.

- **Equal Employment** – The struggle for equal pay and nondiscrimination in employment has resonated throughout the American political economy. The inequality of employment opportunities was especially apparent during the Great Depression and in wartime, when minorities were relegated to substandard jobs and low wages. Women's fight for equal pay, the struggles of minorities in the defense industry, the progress made in employment in New Deal programs, job training for American Indians, the unionization of Hispanic farm workers in the 1960s, and the struggle to accept gays and lesbians in the military are essential to this story. Title VII of the Civil Rights Act of 1964 forbade discrimination by employers and created the Equal Employment Opportunity Commission to investigate discrimination complaints across the nation.

The home of Mary McLeod Bethune, a presidential advisor during the New Deal program, is the one National Historic Landmark associated with this theme. The civil rights overview identifies other important individuals and events such as Betty Friedan and Aileen Hernandez who were nationally influential in gaining equal pay and job opportunities for women, César Chávez and the UFW for their work on farm labor, and the African American drive for equal employment in the 1963 March on Washington. The National Park Service is preparing a National Historic Landmarks theme study entitled *Civil Rights in America: Racial Discrimination in Employment*.

- **Criminal Injustice** – This theme covers multiple topics and minority groups. Anti-Chinese violence in the American West in the mid-to-late-nineteenth century, anti-Mexican violence during the 1940s in Los Angeles, and anti-gay violence and police harassment revealed how minority groups were categorized as antisocial and a menace to society. Another civil rights crime, lynching, took place among both African Americans and Hispanics. Although the numerous lynchings of African Americans have been well documented, it is less well known that persons of Mexican heritage were lynched between 1848 and 1928.

Another injustice was the forced incarceration Japanese Americans experienced in World War II as described in the National Park Service study, *Confinement and Ethnicity: An Overview of World War II Japanese American Relocation Sites* (1999). Its history of Japanese American relocation during the war, provides an overview of the tangible remains of internment sites (eight previously listed in the National Register of Historic Places), and describes existing interpretation. Six of these internment sites have received National Historic Landmark designation, and two sites, Manzanar and Minidoka, are National Park System Units. Information in the *Confinement and Ethnicity* study serves as the basis for the draft National Historic Landmarks theme study *Japanese Americans in World War II* as authorized in the Manzanar National Historic Site enabling legislation.

- **Immigrant Rights** – The mass deportation of millions of Mexicans (and Hispanics) during the 1930s and 1950s signaled an era when basic civil liberties and human rights were abridged in communities swept by the Immigration and Naturalization Service. Organizations such as the Committee for the Protection of the Foreign Born provided assistance to people whose rights were violated. To date, no National Historic Landmark theme study covers this topic.

- **American Indian Civil Rights** – Multiple events, places, and individuals are associated with American Indian civil rights. Some National Historic Landmarks depict this group's unique civil rights history regarding treaties and assimilation. The site where the Choctaw tribe signed a forced treaty that gave up all their claims to land east of the Mississippi River is represented by the Dancing Rabbit Creek Treaty Site National Historic Landmark. The forced removal of Indians east of the Mississippi is represented by sites such as the John Ross House National Historic Landmark and the Trail of Tears National Historic Trail. The American Indian Movement efforts to regain sovereign rights are represented in the 1969-1971 occupation of Alcatraz, a National Park System unit. Other people, events, and places listed in this study's overview may be deserving of evaluation. To date, no National Historic Landmark theme study covers this unique history.

STUDY FINDINGS

The civil rights story depicts one of the greatest struggles in American history, one that continues to this day. The nation's founding documents—the Declaration of Independence and the Constitution—promise equal treatment under the law. The victories that women and minorities have won in their fights for the fulfillment of those promises have improved the social and economic lives of millions of minorities and women and consequently transformed the nation. To tell the civil rights story, therefore, requires that sites related to women and minority groups be identified, preserved, and interpreted.

Based on this study's overview and analysis of existing and potential sites, the following findings are presented. These findings concentrate on themes and minority groups in need of further intensive study to help preserve and interpret sites crucial to the national civil rights movement.

1. **Many civil rights–related sites have been identified and recognized.** National Park Service recognition of the nation's civil rights story is most readily reflected in prominent individuals such as Susan B. Anthony and Martin Luther King, Jr., and well-known events like the desegregation of Little Rock Central High School and the 1965 Selma-to-Montgomery Voting Rights March. Most sites represent the lifetime work of highly

influential activists or pivotal moments in civil rights history. National Historic Landmarks identified in Table 1 include thirty-three associated with African Americans, sixteen with American Indians, fifteen with women, six with Asian Americans, one with Hispanics, and one with the gay and lesbian movement. National Park Service units and National Historic Trails that interpret civil rights include nine associated with African Americans, two with women, two with Asian Americans, and three with American Indians.

2. **A number of civil rights-related sites have not been recognized.** The historians who contributed to this study listed many important events, places, and people in the overview that are not yet evaluated within a theme study. This list is not intended to be comprehensive or definitive, but to help the National Park Service assess how well civil rights sites are represented. Regarding the various minority groups, the inventory of civil rights sites appears limited for Hispanics and Asian Americans, and for American Indians in the New Deal (1934-1945), Termination (1945-1960), and Self-Determination (1960-1975) eras. In regard to historical themes, however, the National Park Service is addressing the topics of public accommodations, equal employment, housing, and voting within theme studies.

STUDY RECOMMENDATIONS

Because some civil rights topics are underrepresented in interpreting our cultures, this study recommends completing four National Historic Landmark theme studies to recognize, promote, and protect civil rights–related sites that meet the National Park Service's thematic framework of "creating social institutions and movements" and "shaping the political landscape." Theme studies assist park planners and historians in identifying sites that may be considered for preservation within the National Park System and National Historic Landmark designation.

1. **Complete chapters of the National Historic Landmarks theme study: *Civil Rights in America*.** Based on four provisions of the 1960s civil rights acts (voting, equal employment, housing, and public accommodations), the *Civil Rights in America* theme study portrays chapters in the nation's civil rights story, each having its own significance within the movement. Every chapter provides a historic context, registration requirements, and a National Historic Landmark study list of properties that have strong associations with nationally significant topics in the civil rights context. Two draft chapters currently available are *Desegregation of Public Accommodations* and *Racial Voting Rights*. The final two chapters in preparation are *Racial Discrimination in Housing* and *Racial Employment Discrimination*. The *Civil Rights in America* theme study accompanies the previously completed theme study, *Racial Desegregation in Public Education in the United States* (2000), a study that has produced eight National Historic Landmark designations.

2. **Subject to available funding, undertake civil rights studies related to other minority groups.** The framework study examined topics related to the history of other minority groups within the United States, including Asian Americans, Hispanics, gays and lesbians, and women, as well as the unique American Indian civil rights story (including

Alaska Natives and Native Hawaiians). Undertaking additional studies will assist National Park Service units with telling the civil rights story related to these groups and identify related sites and individuals relevant to these groups for possible National Historic Landmark nomination

TABLE 1. NATIONAL HISTORIC LANDMARKS AND NATIONAL PARK SYSTEM UNITS BY CIVIL RIGHTS ERAS[14]

AN EMERGING CAUSE, 1776–1865

Site	Theme	Affiliation	Significance
NATIONAL HISTORIC LANDMARKS			
Field House St. Louis, Missouri	All	African American	The Field House was the home of Roswell Field while he was legal counsel for the slave Dred Scott who sued for his freedom in one of the most significant cases in American constitutional history, *Scott v. Sandford* (1857).
William C. Nell Residence Boston, Massachusetts	All	African American	William C. Nell was a leading black abolitionist and spokesman for civil rights from the 1830s to the end of the Civil War.
Margaret Fuller House Cambridge, Massachusetts	Voting	Women	Margaret Fuller was an advocate for women's emancipation. She authored *Woman in the Nineteenth Century* (1845) which is known as "the first considered statement of feminism" in America.
Liberty Farm Worcester, Massachusetts	Voting	Women	From 1847 to 1881, Liberty Farm was the home of reformers Abigail Kelly and her husband Stephen Symonds Foster. The home served as a station on the Underground Railroad. Kelly was one of the first American women to speak out publicly against slavery. The couple also participated in the struggle for women's rights and withheld taxes on the farm to protest Kelly's inability to vote.
Elizabeth Cady Stanton House Seneca Falls, New York	Voting	Women	Elizabeth Cady Stanton, a major figure in the struggle for women's rights who initiated the suffragist movement, lived here. Together with Lucretia Mott, Stanton organized the first women's rights convention held in Seneca Falls in 1848. The house is now the major component of the Women's Rights National Historical Park.
Race Street Meetinghouse Philadelphia, Pennsylvania	Voting	Women	This meetinghouse was at the forefront of women's involvement in both the Quaker religion and American political activism. Many leaders in the women's movement were associated with this meetinghouse, among them abolitionist and activist Lucretia Mott, peace activist Hannah Clothier Hull, and suffrage leader Alice Paul.
NATIONAL PARK SYSTEM UNITS			
Boston African American National Historic Site Boston, Massachusetts	Education	African American	This site contains the Smith School associated with *Robert v. City of Boston* (1849), whereby the Massachusetts Supreme Court established the separate but equal principle.
Women's Rights National Historical Park Seneca Falls, New York	Voting	Women	The park contains the setting of the first Women's Rights Convention (1848) in Wesleyan Chapel and the houses of important participants (including the Elizabeth Cady Stanton NHL), to tell the story of one of the fights for women's equality.

[14] List compiled from *National Landmarks, America's Treasures The National Park Foundation's Complete Guide to National Historic Landmarks*, 2000, under index topics of Civil Rights, Hispanic History, Women's History, Native American History, Asian History, and African American History; National Historic Landmarks Theme Study: *Racial Desegregation in Public Education in the United States*, National Park Service, August 2000; *The U.S. Constitution NHL Theme Study* (1986) under topics of Fifth Amendment Due Process, Fourteenth Amendment Due Process, Racial Discrimination, Miscellaneous, and Civil Rights and the Constitution; The National Parks: Index 2005–2007; and the National Historic Landmarks Web site, searched under the theme of Civil Rights Movements. Compilation of sites is based on the civil rights overview of this framework.

RECONSTRUCTION & REPRESSION, 1865–1900

NATIONAL HISTORIC LANDMARKS

Site	Theme	Affiliation	Significance
Susan B. Anthony House Rochester, New York	Voting	Women	Active in numerous reform movements, Susan B. Anthony entered the fight for women's rights in 1851 after meeting women's rights advocate Elizabeth Cady Stanton. In 1869 she played the leading role in organizing the National Woman Suffrage Association. Anthony lived here from 1866 until her death in 1906.
Elizabeth Cady Stanton House Tenafly, New Jersey	Voting	Women	From about 1868 to 1887, this house was the residence of Elizabeth Cady Stanton, early leader in the woman's rights movement. She spent her most active years working for women's rights in Tenafly.
Kimberly Mansion Glastonbury, Connecticut	Voting	Women	In the 1870s, two elderly sisters, Julia and Abby Smith, attracted international attention to their stand on women's rights when they protested against "taxation without representation" and eventually secured a legal decision against the tax collector on a farmhouse they had inherited.
Wyoming State Capitol Cheyenne, Wyoming	Voting	Women	This state capitol represents Wyoming's achievement in 1890, when it gained statehood and became the first state to grant women full suffrage.
Frances Ellen Watkins Harper House Philadelphia, Pennsylvania	Voting	Women African American	Born of free black parents in 1825, Frances Ellen Watkins Harper became a writer and social activist and participated in the abolitionist, black rights, woman suffrage, and temperance movements. She began her career as an abolitionist spokesperson in 1854. She lived in this house from 1870 until her death in 1911.
Charlotte Forten Grimke House Washington, D.C.	Voting	Women African American	From 1881 to 1886, this was the home of Charlotte Forten Grimke, a pioneer black female educator, early supporter of women's rights, writer and abolitionist.
Mary Church Terrell House Washington, D.C.	Voting	Women African American	Educator and civil rights leader, Mary Church Terrell, was the first black woman to serve on an American school board (1895) and the first president of the National Association of Colored Women.
Pittsylvania County Courthouse Chatham, Virginia	Criminal injustice	African American	In 1880, the U.S. Supreme Court ruled that black citizens who had been denied the right to serve as grand or petit jurors violated the Civil Rights Act of 1875.
Lyman Trumbull House Alton, Illinois	All	African American	This prominent Republican statesman from Illinois chaired the U.S. Senate's Judiciary Committee from 1861 to 1871. He sponsored and secured passage of Reconstruction legislation, including the Freedmen's Bureau Bill and the Civil Rights Act of 1866.

NATIONAL PARK SYSTEM UNIT

Site	Theme	Affiliation	Significance
Frederick Douglass National Historic Site Washington, D.C.	All	African American	Douglass was an early supporter of blacks' and women's rights, a social reformer, and is referred to as the father of the civil rights movement.

REKINDLING CIVIL RIGHTS, 1900-1941

NATIONAL HISTORIC LANDMARKS

Site	Theme	Affiliation	Significance
Rankin Ranch Avalanche Gulch, Montana	Voting	Women	In 1916, Jeanette Rankin was the first woman elected to serve in the U.S. House of Representatives at a time when most states did not allow women to vote. Rankin served two terms, 1917-1919 and 1941-1943, and is best remembered for her pacifism. She also played an important role in women's rights and in the social reform movement.
Paulsdale Mount Laurel Township, New Jersey	Voting	Women	This was the childhood home and permanent "home base" of Alice Paul, a leader in the women's suffrage movement. She drafted the Equal Rights Amendment in the 1920s and worked to secure passage of the Nineteenth Amendment in 1920, giving women the vote.
Sewall-Belmont House Washington, D.C.	Voting	Women	Since 1929, this house has served as the headquarters of the National Woman's Party. (This property is also a National Historic Site.)
Constitution Hall Washington, D.C.	Public Accommodation	African American	This hall, owned by the Daughters of the American Revolution (DAR), served for more than 40 years as an unofficial cultural center for the nation's capitol. The DAR denied use of this hall to singer Marian Anderson in 1939, a notable event in the national struggle for civil rights.
Ida B. Wells-Barnett House Chicago, Illinois	All	Women African American	Ida B. Wells-Barnett was an African American teacher, journalist, and civil rights activist from 1919 to 1929, who, almost single-handedly awakened the world's conscience to the horrible realities of lynching. The cause was afterward taken up by the NAACP, which she had helped organize.
T. Thomas Fortune House Red Bank, New Jersey	All	African American	During the early 20th century, this was the home of crusading journalist T. Thomas Fortune. Born a slave, he articulated the cause of African American rights and provided a national forum for black causes in his newspapers.
William Monroe Trotter House Boston, Massachusetts	All	African American	This was the home of noted African American journalist and militant civil rights activist William Monroe Trotter during the first decades of the 20th century.
Mary McLeod Bethune Home Daytona Beach, Florida	All	African American	Mary McLeod Bethune was an early 20th century African American civil rights advocate, administrator, educator, adviser to presidents, and consultant to the United Nations. She built this house in 1920 and resided there until her death in 1955.
W. E. B. Du Bois Boyhood Homesite Great Barrington vicinity, Massachusetts	All	African American	Du Bois was a prominent sociologist, writer, and major civil rights figure in the first half of the 20th century. From 1928 to 1954, he owned a house here, which is now marked only by ruins.

NATIONAL PARK SYSTEM UNITS

Site	Theme	Affiliation	Significance
Sewall-Belmont House National Historic Site Washington, D.C.	Voting	Women	Since 1929, this house has served as the headquarters of the National Woman's Party. (This property is also a National Historic Landmark.)
Mary McLeod Bethune Council House Washington, D.C.	All	African American	This was the last official Washington, D.C. residence of Mary McLeod Bethune and the first headquarters of the National Council of Negro Women.
Booker T. Washington National Monument Rocky Mount, Virginia	All	African American	This site includes Booker T. Washington's birthplace. After his "Atlanta Compromise" address in 1895 called for blacks to accept segregation in return for future economic opportunity, Washington emerged as the premiere national African American leader.

BIRTH OF THE CIVIL RIGHTS MOVEMENT, 1941-1954

NATIONAL HISTORIC LANDMARKS

Site	Theme	Affiliation	Significance
Manzanar War Relocation Center Lone Pine Vicinity, California	Criminal Injustice	Japanese American	Manzanar was the first of ten internment camps in which people of Japanese descent, most of them Americans, were interned during World War II as a security measure against feared sabotage and espionage under the terms of Executive Order 9066. (Manzanar is also a National Historic Site.)
Tule Lake Segregation Center Newell, California	Criminal Injustice	Japanese American	Tule Lake was the largest and longest-lived of the ten camps built by the civilian War Relocation Authority (WRA) to house Japanese Americans relocated from the West Coast of the United States.
Granada Relocation Center Granada, Colorado	Criminal Injustice	Japanese American	Granada was one of ten camps built by the WRA for incarcerating Japanese Americans during World War II.
Heart Mountain Relocation Center Ralston, Wyoming	Criminal Injustice	Japanese American	Heart Mountain was one of ten facilities built by the WRA for incarcerating Japanese Americans during World War II.
Central Utah Relocation Center Site (Topaz) Delta, Utah	Criminal Injustice	Japanese American	Commonly known as "Topaz," this site is one of ten relocation centers built to intern Japanese Americans during World War II.
Rohwer Relocation Center Cemetery, Rohwer vicinity, Arkansas	Criminal Injustice	Japanese American	Rohwer was one of the ten relocation camps built to intern Japanese Americans during World War II.
Woodmont Gladwyne, Pennsylvania	All	African American	A charismatic African American preacher, the Reverend M. F. Divine had great success in breaking down color lines and fostered integration long before the national civil rights movement. In 1952, Divine made his home at Woodmont.
Shelley House St. Louis, Missouri	Housing	African American	Shelley House is the home of the plaintiffs in *Shelley v. Kramer* (1948), in which the U.S. Supreme Court ruled that enforcement of racially restrictive housing covenants was unconstitutional.
Andrew Rankin Memorial Chapel, Founders Library, and Frederick Douglass Memorial Hall, Howard University, Washington, D.C.	Education	African American	These buildings are associated with Thurgood Marshall and the school desegregation strategy formulated by the NAACP Legal Defense and Educational Fund between 1930 and 1955 that successfully led to overturning the separate but equal doctrine in public education.
Bizzell Library University of Oklahoma Norman, Oklahoma	Education	African American	In *McLaurin v. Oklahoma State Regents for Higher Education* (1950), the U.S. Supreme Court ruled that the University of Oklahoma must treat students equally following admission regardless of race, thereby making separate but equal unattainable in graduate and professional education. In Bizzell Library, the university forced African American student George McLaurin to sit separate from white students.
Howard High School Wilmington, Delaware	Education	African American	Howard High School was the black school in *Belton v. Gebhart* (1953) that was combined with other public school segregation cases in *Brown v. Board of Education* (1954) in which the U.S. Supreme Court found racial segregation in public schools unconstitutional. *Belton* was one of the cases representing the Court's view that segregation existed outside the South.

BIRTH OF THE CIVIL RIGHTS MOVEMENT, 1941-1954 (cont'd.)

Site	Theme	Affiliation	Significance
Sumner Elementary School and Monroe Elementary School Topeka, Kansas	Education	African American	These schools are associated with the public school segregation cases consolidated in *Brown v. Board of Education* (1954) in which the U.S. Supreme Court found segregated schools unconstitutional. Sumner was the segregated white school that denied Oliver Brown the right to enroll his daughter Linda who attended Monroe, the segregated black school. (Monroe Elementary School is also included in the Brown v. Board of Education National Historic Site)
Robert Russa Moton High School Farmville, Virginia	Education	African American	In 1951, black students at Moton High School went on strike to protest conditions at their segregated school. Their court case became one of the cases consolidated in *Brown v. Board of Education* (1954). The school is also associated with Virginia's "massive resistance" to school integration when the county closed all its public schools from 1959 to 1964.
John Philip Sousa Junior High School Washington, D.C.	Education	African American	In a companion case to *Brown v. Board of Education* (1954), the U.S. Supreme Court found segregation at this all-white school in the nation's capital city unconstitutional under the due process clause of the Fifth Amendment, rather than the equal protection clause of the Fourteenth Amendment governing states.
NATIONAL PARK SYSTEM UNITS			
Manzanar National Historic Site Lone Pine Vicinity, California	Criminal Injustice	Japanese American	Manzanar is the first of ten internment camps in which people of Japanese descent, most of them American citizens, were taken from their West Coast homes as a security measure against possible sabotage and espionage during World War II. (Manzanar is also a National Historic Landmark)
Minidoka Internment National Monument Jerome County, Idaho	Criminal Injustice	Japanese American	Minidoka was a relocation center for Japanese Americans during World War II.
Brown v. Board of Education National Historic Site Topeka, Kansas	Education	African American	This site consists of one of the four segregated schools, Monroe Elementary School, (also a National Historic Landmark) for African American children in Topeka and is associated with the U.S. Supreme Court's 1954 decision that segregated schools were unconstitutional.
Tuskegee Airmen National Historic Site Tuskegee, Alabama	Education	African American	Moton Airfield, a hangar, and other buildings at this site are where the Tuskegee Airmen received their initial flight training during World War II. The site commemorates the struggle of African Americans for the right to equal service in the U.S. armed forces.

MODERN CIVIL RIGHTS MOVEMENT, 1954-1964

NATIONAL HISTORIC LANDMARKS

Site	Affiliation	Theme	Significance
Martin Luther King, Jr., Historic District Atlanta, Georgia	African American	All	This district honors the nation's most prominent leader in the 20th century struggle for civil rights. (The district is also a National Historic Site.)
Dexter Avenue Baptist Church Montgomery, Alabama	African American	Public Accommodation	This church played a pivotal role in the 1950s struggle for civil rights. After Rosa Parks was arrested for refusing to sit in the back of a city bus, church pastor Martin Luther King, Jr., helped organize the Montgomery Improvement Association, which held its meetings in the church and successfully boycotted the city's buses in 1955.
Bethel Baptist Church, Parsonage and Guardhouse Birmingham, Alabama	African American	Public Accommodation	These buildings are significant in the evolution of the 1950s church-led southern civil rights movement. From 1956-1961, the Alabama Christian Movement for Human Rights (ACMHR), headquartered in the church, confronted multiple aspects of racial discrimination that served as a model for the 1963 Birmingham campaign. The ACMHR was also pivotal to the 1961 Freedom Ride that compelled the federal government to enforce the desegregation of interstate public transportation and facilities.
Sixteenth Street Baptist Church Birmingham, Alabama	African American	Public Accommodation / Employment	Civil rights marchers assembled here for the 1963 protests in which Public Safety Commissioner "Bull" Conner attacked marchers with fire hoses and police dogs. Also, on September 18, 1963, KKK members bombed the church, killing four girls in Sunday school. These events shocked the nation's conscience, prompted the Kennedy administration to intervene, and contributed to the passage of the Civil Rights Act of 1964.
Dorchester Academy Boys' Dormitory Midway, Georgia	African American	Voting	Dorchester Academy was the primary training site and headquarters for the Citizen Education Program of the Southern Christian Leadership Conference between 1961 and 1970. The program educated disfranchised Southern blacks about their citizenship rights and prepared them for voter registration tests.
Little Rock Central High School Little Rock, Arkansas	African American	Education	In September 1957, the Eisenhower administration enforced court-ordered desegregation at this school in the first such action following the Supreme Court's 1954 *Brown v. Board of Education* decision that segregated public schools were unconstitutional. (This property is also a National Historic Site.)
Daisy Bates House Little Rock, Arkansas	African American	Education	Activist Daisy Bates played an exemplary role in school desegregation. She was influential as the president of the local NAACP and guided the attendance of the Little Rock Nine at Central High School from her home.
Lyceum-The Circle Historic District University of Mississippi Oxford, Mississippi	African American	Education	Between September 30 and October 1, 1962, the Kennedy administration enforced court-ordered desegregation at this university. The tumultuous event marked a decisive turning point in the federal government's enforcement of school desegregation and the decline of violent southern massive resistance to school desegregation.
Foster Auditorium University of Alabama Tuscaloosa, Alabama	African American	Education	This was the site of Governor George Wallace's 1963 "stand in the schoolhouse door" to prevent the registration of black students at the university. On June 11, 1963, after two black students had been admitted, President John F. Kennedy's televised address appealed to Americans for their sense of fairness and recommended congressional civil rights legislation.

MODERN CIVIL RIGHTS MOVEMENT, 1954-1964 (cont'd.)

NATIONAL PARK SYSTEM UNITS

Site	Theme	Affiliation	Significance
Little Rock Central High School National Historic Site Little Rock, Arkansas	Education	African American	In September 1957, the Eisenhower administration enforced court-ordered desegregation at this school in the first such action following the Supreme Court's 1954 *Brown v. Board of Education* decision that segregated public schools were unconstitutional. (This property is also a National Historic Landmark.)
Martin Luther King, Jr., National Historic Site Atlanta, Georgia	All	African American	This site honors Martin Luther King, Jr., the most prominent leader in the 20th century struggle for civil rights. The district includes King's birthplace, the church he pastored, and his grave. (This district is also a National Historic Landmark.)

THE SECOND REVOLUTION, 1964-1976

NATIONAL HISTORIC LANDMARKS

Site	Theme	Affiliation	Significance
Brown Chapel African Methodist Episcopal Church Selma, Alabama	Voting	African American	This chapel played a major role in events leading to passage of the Voting Rights Act of 1965. It was the headquarters of the Selma Voting Rights Movement and the starting point for the three Selma to Montgomery marches.
Church of the Advocate Philadelphia, Pennsylvania	All	African American	This church promoted extensive social reform and embraced the causes of civil rights. It housed the third annual National Conference on Black Power in 1968 and the first ordination of women in the Episcopal Church in 1974.
New Kent Middle School and George Watkins School New Kent County, Virginia	Education	African American	After reviewing the dual school systems at these schools, the U.S. Supreme Court in *Green v. County School Board of New Kent County* (1968) established factors that lower courts would use in determining whether a school had achieved a unitary system. The decision was a critically defining moment when racial desegregation became integration.
Stonewall Greenwich Village, New York	Public Accommodation	Gay & Lesbian	This is the site of the 1969 riot that traditionally marks the beginning of the gay liberation movement and represents the struggle for gay civil rights in America.
Forty Acres Delano, California	Equal Employment	Hispanic	Forty Acres represents the legacy of both the preeminent leader of the Chicano movement, César Chávez, and the United Farm Workers of America, the first permanent agricultural labor union in the U.S. that attained better working conditions for Mexican-American and Filipino agricultural workers.

NATIONAL PARK SYSTEM UNIT

Site	Theme	Affiliation	Significance
Selma to Montgomery National Historic Trail Alabama	Voting	African American	The march from Selma to Montgomery in March 1965 represents the political and emotional peak of the struggle for the right to vote during the modern civil rights movement. The march helped inspire passage of voting rights legislation signed by President Johnson on August 6, 1965.

NATIONAL HISTORIC LANDMARKS

Site	Significance
Dancing Rabbit Creek Treaty Site Macon vicinity, Mississippi	On September 27, 1830, the Choctaw tribe signed a forced treaty at this gathering place. The treaty gave up all claims to land east of the Mississippi River and ultimately led to the tribe's removal. The treaty later served as a model for similar pacts of removal for the Chickasaw, Cherokee, Creek, and Seminole nations.
Fort Mitchell Site Phenix City vicinity, Alaska	Associated with the Creek Indian Nation, this site symbolizes three policies relating to American Indians during the early 19th century: 1) the period of land concessions, 2) federal government attempts to honor treaty obligations, and 3) the Indian Removal policy of the 1830s.
Chieftains Rome, Georgia	Cherokee leader Major Ridge resided here sometime before 1819 to 1838. Ridge was a speaker of the Cherokee National Council and advocate of assimilating Anglo-American culture. On December 29, 1835, he signed the Treaty of New Echota leading to the removal of the Cherokees on the "Trail of Tears."
John Ross House Rossville, Georgia	This was the home of the chief of the Cherokee nation. Ross protested the removal of his people from their ancestral lands and eventually led his people into forced exile from east of the Mississippi along the "Trail of Tears."
New Echota Grodon, Georgia	This first national capital of the Cherokees, established in 1825, was based on an Anglo American precedent. The Treaty of New Echota was signed here, establishing the basic pretext for the final removal of the Cherokee to the west along the "Trail of Tears."
Fort King Ocala, Florida	Originally constructed in 1827, Fort King relates to the Indian removal policies associated with Jacksonian Democracy.
Medicine Lodge Peace Treaty Site Medicine Lodge vicinity, Kansas	In October 1867, U.S. Commissioners met with members of various southern Plains tribes to forge a peace treaty under which the Indians gave up their nomadic life in exchange for permanent reservations in Indian territory and the U.S. government agreed to provide assistance.

NATIONAL PARK SYSTEM UNITS[15]

Site	Significance
Horseshoe Bend National Military Park Alabama	This 2,040-acre park preserves the site of the battle between General Andrew Jackson and Upper Creek or Red Stick warriors on March 27, 1814, at the "horseshoe" bend of the Tallapoosa River, when Jackson's forces broke the power of the Upper Creek Indian Confederacy. A peace treaty signed after the battle forced the Upper and Lower Creeks to give the U.S. nearly 20 million acres of land that opened large parts of Alabama and Georgia to settlement.
Trail of Tears National Historic Trail	This 2,200-mile trail commemorates the route more than 16,000 Cherokee Indians traveled on a forced exile from their ancestral lands in Alabama, Georgia, North Carolina, and Tennessee to Indian Territory west of the Mississippi River in 1838-1839.

[15] Many National Park System units and National Historic Landmarks are significant for their association with the federal government and American Indians during this era. Listed here are those associated directly with treaties and federal government policies relating to American Indians. Other units and landmarks significant for their association with peacekeeping efforts, military bases of operations, Indian Agency sites, non-treaty or short-lived treaty events, and battles in which tribes lost or sold land may warrant inclusion in an American Indian civil rights study.

ASSIMILATION AND ALLOTMENT ERA, 1871-1934

NATIONAL HISTORIC LANDMARKS

Site	Significance
Sheldon Jackson School Sitka, Alaska	This school is nationally significant for its important role in the education of Native Alaskans and the transformation of Southeast Native Alaskan culture during the first half of the 20th century. Changes in Native Alaskan life were instigated by the removal of native students form their homes to the school with the goal of permanently removing them from the Native community.
Carlisle Indian School Carlisle, Pennsylvania	This boarding school pioneered federal education programs for American Indians. The school became a model for similar facilities whose programs were based on the premise of "civilizing" Indians into white man's ways.
Haskell Institute Lawrence, Kansas	Founded in 1884, Haskell was one of the first large off-reservation boarding schools established by the federal government for Indian students.
Cherokee National Capitol Tahlequah, Oklahoma	This building served as the council meeting place of the Cherokee National Council from 1869 until 1907, when Oklahoma became a state, and stands as a symbol of the Cherokee's ability to adjust their culture to prevailing customs.
Creek National Capitol Okmulgee, Oklahoma	This 1878 building served as the meeting place of the Creek Indian Council. The Creek Nation's government is modeled on that of the U.S. government. The building's design accommodated two legislative houses and a Supreme Court.
George C. Thomas Memorial Library Fairbanks, Alaska	This log structure was the site of a 1915 meeting between U.S. government officials and Native Alaskans to settle land and compensation claims. The meeting started a dispute that was not resolved until passage of the Alaska Native Claims Settlement Act of 1971.
Chief Plenty Coups Home Big Horn County, Montana	Chief of the Crow people, Plenty Coups advocated adopting those aspects of American culture necessary to succeed on the reservation while maintaining traditional religious beliefs and cultural values.
Alaska Native Brotherhood Hall Baranof Island, Alaska	Built in 1914, the Alaska Native Brotherhood/Sisterhood Society built this meeting hall. The group achieved many civil rights victories including the right to Workmen's Compensation, the right of native children to attend school, and in 1929 initiated the first native claims court suit leading to the Alaska Native Claims Settlement Act of 1971.

INDIAN NEW DEAL ERA, 1934-1945

NATIONAL HISTORIC LANDMARK

Site	Significance
Navajo Nation Council Chamber Window Rock, Arizona	The Council Chamber symbolizes the New Deal revolution in federal Indian policy. Completed in 1936, the building was designed to stand in declaration of economic and cultural self-determination as afforded to Native Americans by the Indian Reorganization Act of 1934. The act sought to advocate the reconstitution of tribal organization, the restoration of a tribal land base, and the promotion of traditional Indian culture.

SELF-DETERMINATION ERA, 1960-1975

NATIONAL PARK SYSTEM UNIT

Site	Significance
Alcatraz Island Part of Golden Gate National Recreation Area San Francisco, California	The American Indian occupation of Alcatraz from 1969 to 1971 marked the change from termination to self-determination for Indian governments.

BIBLIOGRAPHY

GENERAL SOURCES

Foner, Eric. *The Story of American Freedom.* New York: W. W. Norton & Company, 1998.

Graham, Hugh Davis. "The Civil Rights Commission: The First 40 Years." *Civil Rights Journal* (Fall 1997): 6-8.

Grossman, Mark. *The ABC-CLIO Companion to the Civil Rights Movement.* Santa Barbara: ABC-CLIO, 1993.

Hall, Kermit L., ed. *Race Relations and the Law in American History: Major Historical Interpretations.* New York: Garland Publishing Co., 1987.

Kellog, Peter J. "Civil Rights Consciousness in the 1940s." In *Civil Rights in American History: Major Historical Interpretations*, ed. Kermit L. Hall. New York: Garland Publishing, Inc., 1987.

Loevy, Robert D., ed. *The Civil Rights Act of 1964: The Passage of the Law That Ended Racial Segregation.* Albany: State University of New York Press, 1997.

Olson, James S., ed. *Encyclopedia of American Indian Civil Rights.* Westwood, CT: Greenwood Press, 1977.

Safire, William. *Safire's New Political Dictionary: The Definitive Guide to the New Language of Politics.* New York: Random House, 1993.

Sigler, Jay A. *Civil Rights in America: 1500 to the Present.* Detroit: Gale, 1998.

RECOMMENDED READING

African American

<u>Education:</u>

Ashmore, Harry S. *The Negro and the Schools*. Chapel Hill: University of North Carolina Press, 1954.

Ball, Howard. *The Bakke Case: Race, Education, and Affirmative Action*. Lawrence: University Press of Kansas, 2000.

Bond, Horace Mann. *Negro Education in Alabama: A Study in Cotton and Steel*. Washington, DC: The Associated Publishers, 1939.

Bullock, Henry Allen. *A History of Negro Education in the South: From 1619 to the Present*. Cambridge, MA: Harvard University Press, 1967.

Duram, James C. *A Moderate Among Extremists: Dwight D. Eisenhower and the School Desegregation Crisis*. Chicago: Nelson-Hall, 1981.

Fairclough, Adam. *A Class of Their Own: Black Teachers in the Segregated South*. Cambridge, MA: Belknap Press of Harvard University Press, 2007.

————. *Teaching Equality: Black Schools in the Age of Jim Crow*. Athens: University of Georgia Press, 2001.

Harlan, Louis R. *Separate and Unequal: Public School Campaigns and Racism in the Southern Seaboard States, 1901-1915*. Chapel Hill: University of North Carolina Press, 1958.

Kluger, Richard. *Simple Justice: The History of Brown v. Board of Education and Black America's Struggle for Equality*. New York: Knopf, 1975.

Kousser, J. Morgan. "Separate but *not* Equal: The Supreme Court's First Decision on Racial Discrimination in Schools." *Journal of Southern History* 46, No. 1 (February 1980): 17-44.

Tushnet, Mark V. *The NAACP's Legal Strategy Against Segregated Education, 1925-1950*. Chapel Hill: University of North Carolina Press, 1987.

Wilkinson, J. Harvie. *From Brown to Bakke: The Supreme Court and School Integration, 1954-1978*. New York: Oxford University Press, 1979.

Williams, Juan. *Thurgood Marshall, American Revolutionary*. New York: Times Books, 1998.

Equal Employment:

Arnesen, Eric. *Brotherhoods of Color: Black Railroad Workers and the Struggle for Equality.* Cambridge, MA: Harvard University Press, 2001.

Boggs, James. *Racism and the Class Struggle: Further Pages from a Black Worker's Notebook.* New York: Monthly Review Press, 1970.

Brazeal, Brailsford R. *The Brotherhood of Sleeping Car Porters.* New York: Harper and Brothers, 1946.

Burstein, Paul. *Discrimination, Jobs, and Politics: The Struggle for Equal Employment Opportunity in the United States Since the New Deal.* Chicago: University of Chicago Press, 1985.

Foner, Philip S., and Ronald L. Lewis, eds. *The Black Worker: A Documentary History from Colonial Times to the Present.* Philadelphia: Temple University Press, 1989.

Garfinkel, Herbert. *When Negroes March: The March on Washington Movement in the Organizational Politics for FEPC.* Glencoe, IL: Free Press, 1959.

Gould, William B. *Black Workers in White Unions: Job Discrimination in the United States.* Ithaca: Cornell University Press, 1977.

Kesselman, Louis C. *The Social Politics of FEPC.* Chapel Hill: University of North Carolina Press, 1948.

Marable, Manning. *Black Liberation in Conservative America.* Boston: South End Press, 1997.

Nelson, Bruce. *Divided We Stand: American Workers and the Struggle for Black Equality.* Princeton: Princeton University Press, 2001.

Report of the National Advisory Commission on Civil Disorders. Washington, DC: U.S. Government Printing Office, 1968.

Weaver, Robert C. *Negro Labor: A National Problem.* New York: Harcourt, Brace, and Co., 1946.

Public Accommodations:

Chafe, William H. *Civilities and Civil Rights: Greensboro, North Carolina, and the Black Struggle for Freedom.* New York: Oxford University Press, 1980.

Manis, Andrew M. *A Fire You Can't Put Out: The Civil Rights Life of Birmingham's Reverend Fred Shuttlesworth.* Tuscaloosa: University of Alabama Press, 1999.

Morris, Aldon D. *The Origins of the Civil Rights Movement: Black Communities Organizing for Change.* New York: Free Press, 1984.

Rabinowitz, Howard N. *Race Relations in the Urban South, 1865-1890.* New York: Oxford University Press, 1978.

Rabby, Glenda. *The Pain and the Promise: The Struggle for Civil Rights in Tallahassee, Florida.* Athens: University of Georgia Press, 1999.

Woodward, C. Vann. *The Strange Career of Jim Crow.* Commemorative ed. New York: Oxford University Press, 2002.

Wynes, Charles E. *Race Relations in Virginia, 1870-1902.* Charlottesville: University Press of Virginia, 1961.

Voting Rights:

Dailey, Jane, Glenda Elizabeth Gilmore, and Bryant Simon, eds. *Jumpin' Jim Crow: Southern Politics from Civil War to Civil Rights.* Princeton: Princeton University Press, 2000.

De Santis, Vincent P. *Republicans Face the Southern Question: The New Departure Years, 1877-1897.* Baltimore: Johns Hopkins Press, 1959.

Garrow, David J. *Protest at Selma: Martin Luther King, Jr., and the Voting Rights Act of 1965.* New Haven: Yale University Press, 1978.

Hamilton, Charles V. *The Bench and the Ballot: Southern Federal Judges and Black Votes.* New York: Oxford University Press, 1973.

Hine, Darlene Clark. *Black Victory: The Rise and Fall of the White Primary in Texas.* Millwood, NY: KTO Press, 1979.

Kirwan, Albert D. *Revolt of the Rednecks: Mississippi Politics, 1876-1925.* Lexington: University of Kentucky Press, 1951.

Kousser, J. Morgan. *The Shaping of Southern Politics: Suffrage Restriction and the Establishment of the One-Party South, 1880-1910.* New Haven: Yale University Press, 1974.

Lawson, Steven F. *Black Ballots: Voting Rights in the South, 1944-1969.* New York: Columbia University Press, 1976.

Perman, Michael. *Struggle for Mastery: Disfranchisement in the South, 1888-1908.* Chapel Hill: University of North Carolina Press, 2001.

Multiple Themes:

Branch, Taylor. *Parting the Waters: America in the King Years, 1954-1963.* New York: Simon and Schuster, 1988.

———. *Pillar of Fire: America in the King Years, 1963-1965.* New York: Simon and Schuster, 1998.

———. *At Canaan's Edge: America in the King Years, 1965-1968.* New York: Simon and Schuster, 2006.

Dittmer, John. *Local People: The Struggle for Civil Rights in Mississippi.* Urbana: University of Illinois Press, 1994.

Fairclough, Adam. *Better Day Coming: Blacks and Equality, 1890-2000.* New York: Viking, 2001.

Graham, Hugh Davis. *The Civil Rights Era: Origins and Development of National Policy, 1960-1972.* New York: Oxford University Press, 1990.

Howard, John R. *The Shifting Wind: The Supreme Court and Civil Rights from Reconstruction to Brown.* Albany: State University of New York Press, 1999.

Lehmann, Nicholas. *Promised Land: The Great Black Migration and How it Changed America.* New York: Alfred A. Knopf, 1991.

———. *Redemption: The Last Battle of the Civil War.* New York: Farrar, Straus, and Giroux, 2006.

Logan, Rayford. *The Betrayal of the Negro, from Rutherford B. Hayes to Woodrow Wilson.* New York: Collier Books, 1965.

Whalen, Charles W. and Barbara. *The Longest Debate: A Legislative History of the 1964 Civil Rights Act.* Cabin John, MD: Seven Locks Press, 1985.

Williams, Patricia J. *The Alchemy of Race and Rights.* Cambridge, MA: Harvard University Press, 1991.

Young, Andrew. *An Easy Burden: The Civil Rights Movement and the Transformation of America.* New York: HarperCollins Publishers, 1996.

Asian American

Ancheta, Angelo N. *Race, Rights, and the Asian American Experience.* New Brunswick: Rutgers University Press, 1998.

Chan, Sucheng, ed. *Entry Denied: Exclusion and the Chinese Community in America, 1882–1943*. Philadelphia: Temple University Press, 1991.

—————. *Asian Americans: An Interpretive History*. Boston: Twayne Publishers, 1991.

Chen, Yong. *Chinese San Francisco, 1850-1943: A Trans-Pacific Community*. Stanford: Stanford University Press, 2000.

Cheng, Lucie, and Edna Bonacich, eds. *Labor Immigration under Capitalism: Asian Workers in the United States before World War II*. Berkeley: University of California Press, 1984.

Cordova, Fred. *Filipinos: Forgotten Asian Americans: A Pictorial Essay, 1763-circa 1963*. Dubuque, IA: Kendall/Hunt Pub. Co., 1983.

Daniels, Roger, ed. *Anti-Chinese Violence in North America*. New York: Arno Press, 1978.

—————. *Concentration Camps USA: Japanese Americans and World War II*. New York: Holt, Rinehart and Winston, 1971.

Foner, Philip S., and Daniel Rosenberg, eds. *Racism, Dissent, and Asian Americans from 1850 to the Present: A Documentary History*. Westport, CT: Greenwood Press, 1993.

Friday, Chris. *Organizing Asian American Labor: The Pacific Coast Canned-Salmon Industry, 1870-1942*. Philadelphia: Temple University Press, 1994.

Gyory, Andrew. *Closing the Gate: Race, Politics, and the Chinese Exclusion Act*. Chapel Hill: University of North Carolina Press, 1998.

Hatamiya, Leslie T. *Righting a Wrong: Japanese Americans and the Passage of the Civil Liberties Act of 1988*. Stanford: Stanford University Press, 1993.

Jensen, Joan M. *Passage from India: Asian Indian Immigrants in North America*. New Haven: Yale University Press, 1988.

Kim, Hyung-chan, ed. *Asian Americans and the Supreme Court: A Documentary History*. New York: Greenwood Press, 1992.

McClain, Charles, ed. *Asian Indians, Filipinos, Other Asian Communities, and the Law*. New York: Garland Pub., 1994.

Odo, Franklin, ed. *The Columbia Documentary History of the Asian American Experience*. New York: Columbia University Press, 2002.

Okihiro, Gary Y. *Margins and Mainstreams: Asians in American History and Culture*. Seattle: University of Washington Press, 1994.

Hing, Bill Ong. *Making and Remaking Asian America through Immigration Policy, 1850–1990.* Stanford: Stanford University Press, 1993.

Takaki, Ronald. *Strangers from a Different Shore: A History of Asian Americans.* Boston: Little, Brown, 1998.

Yung, Judy. *Unbound Feet: A Social History of Chinese Women in San Francisco.* Berkeley: University of California Press, 1995.

Gay/Lesbian

Alsenas, Linas. *Gay America: Struggle for Equality.* New York: Amulet Books, 2008.

Bérubé, Allan. *Coming Out Under Fire: The History of Gay Men and Women in World War II.* New York: Free Press, 1990.

Boyd, Nan Alamilla. "'Homos Invade S.F.!' San Francisco's History as a Wide-Open Town." In *Creating a Place for Ourselves: Lesbian, Gay, and Bisexual Community Histories*, edited by Brett Beemyn. New York: Routledge, 1997.

Bullough, Vern L., ed. *Before Stonewall: Activists for Gay and Lesbian Rights in Historical Context.* New York: Harrington Park Press, 2002.

Carter, David. *Stonewall: The Riots that Sparked the Gay Revolution.* New York: St. Martin's Press, 2004.

D'Emilio, John. *Sexual Politics, Sexual Communities: The Making of a Homosexual Minority in the United States, 1940-1970.* Chicago, IL: University of Chicago Press, 1983.

Duberman, Martin Bauml. *Stonewall.* New York: Dutton, 1993.

Eisenbach, David. *Gay Power: An American Revolution.* New York: Carroll & Graf, 2006.

Epstein, Steven. "Gay and Lesbian Movements in the United States: Dilemmas of Identity, Diversity, and Political Strategy." In *The Global Emergence of Gay and Lesbian Politics: National Imprints of a Worldwide Movement*, ed. Barry D. Adam, Jan Willem Duyvendak, and André Krouwel. Philadelphia, PA: Temple University Press, 1999.

History Project, The. *Improper Bostonians: Lesbian and Gay History from the Puritans to Playland.* Boston, MA: Beacon Press, 1998.

Katz, Jonathan Ned. *Gay American History.* New York: Thomas Y. Crowell, 1976.

———. *Gay/Lesbian Almanac: A New Documentary.* New York: Harper and Row, 1983.

Kennedy, Elizabeth Lapovsky, and Madeline D. Davis. *Boots of Leather, Slippers of Gold: The History of a Lesbian Community*. New York: Routledge, 1993.

Kissack, Terrance. "Freaking Fag Revolutionaries: New York's Gay Liberation Front, 1969-1971." *Radical History Review* 62 (1995): 104–34.

Marcus, Eric. *Making Gay History: The Half-Century Fight for Lesbian and Gay Equal Rights*. New York: Perennial, 2002.

McGarry, Molly, and Fred Wasserman. *Becoming Visible: An Illustrated History of Lesbian and Gay Life in Twentieth-Century America*. New York: Penguin Studio, 1998.

Myers, JoAnne. *Historical Dictionary of the Lesbian Liberation Movement: Still the Rage*. Lanham, MD: Scarecrow Press, 2003.

Nestle, Joan. "Butch-Fem Relationships: Sexual Courage in the 1950s." *Heresies* 3, no. 4 (1981): 21-24.

Rupp, Leila J. *A Desired Past: A Short History of Same-Sex Love in America*. Chicago: University of Chicago Press, 1999.

Sears, James T. *Behind the Mask of the Mattachine: The Hal Call Chronicles and the Early Movement for Homosexual Emancipation*. New York: Harrington Park Press, c2006.

Stein, Marc. *City of Sisterly and Brotherly Loves: Lesbian and Gay Philadelphia, 1945-1972*. Chicago: University of Chicago Press, 2000.

Thompson, Mark, ed. *Long Road to Freedom: The Advocate History of the Gay and Lesbian Movement*. New York: St. Martin's, 1994.

Hispanic

Mariscal, George. *Brown-Eyed Children of the Sun: Lessons from the Chicano Movement, 1965–1975*. Albuquerque: University of New Mexico Press, 2005.

Meier, Matt S., and Margo Gutiérrez. *Encyclopedia of the Mexican American Civil Rights Movement*. Westport, CT: Greenwood Press, 2000.

Muñoz, Carlos, Jr. *Youth, Identity, Power: The Chicano Movement*. Rev. and expanded ed. New York: Verso, 2007.

Rosales, F. Arturo. *Chicano! The History of the Mexican American Civil Rights Movement*. Houston, TX: Arte Publico Press, 1996.

American Indian

Burnett, Donald L., Jr. "An Historical Analysis of the 1968 'Indian Civil Rights' Act." In *Civil Rights in American History: Major Historical Interpretations*. New York: Garland Publishing Inc., 1987. First appeared in *Harvard Journal on Legislation* 9 (May 1972): 557-626.

Champagne, Duane, ed. *Native America: Portrait of the Peoples*. Detroit, MI: Invisible Ink Press, 1994.

————. *American Indian Societies: Strategies and Conditions of Political and Cultural Survival*. Cambridge, MA: Cultural Survival, Inc., 1989.

Cobb, Daniel M., and Loretta Fowler, eds. *Beyond Red Power: American Indian Politics and Activism Since 1900*. Santa Fe, NM: School for Advanced Research, 2007.

Deloria, Vine, Jr. *Behind the Trail of Broken Treaties: An Indian Declaration of Independence*. New York: Delacorte Publishing, 1974.

———— and Clifford M. Lytle. *American Indians, American Justice*. Austin: University of Texas Press, 1983.

Edmunds, R. David. *American Indian Leaders: Studies in Diversity*. Lincoln: University of Nebraska Press, 1980.

Johnson, Troy R. *Red Power: The Native American Civil Rights Movement*. New York: Chelsea House, 2007.

Josephy, Alvin M. *Now That the Buffalo's Gone: A Study of Today's American Indians*. New York: Knopf, 1982.

Klaus, Frantz. *Indian Reservations in the United States: Territory, Sovereignty, and Socioeconomic Change*. Chicago: University of Chicago Press, 1999.

Kukathas, Uma. *Native American Rights*. Detroit, MI: Greenhaven Press, 2008.

McCool, Daniel, Susan M. Olson, and Jennifer L. Robinson. *Native Vote: American Indians, the Voting Rights Act, and the Right to Vote*. New York: Cambridge University Press, 2007.

Olson, James S. ed. *Encyclopedia of American Indian Civil Rights*. Westport, CT: Greenwood Press, 1997.

Strange, Carolyn, and Tina Loo. "Holding the Rock: The 'Indianization' of Alcatraz Island, 1969–1999." *The Public Historian* 23, No. 1 (Winter 2001): 55-74.

Townsend, Charles P., ed. *Native Americans: Rights, Laws, and Legislative Developments*. New York: Nova Science Publishers, 2008.

Vaughn, Sam. "Civil and Human Rights Interpretive Planning Workshop Proceedings." Atlanta, GA: National Park Service, December 9-10, 1997.

Weeks, Philip, ed. *They Made Us Many Promises: The American Indian Experience, 1524 to the Present.* 2nd. ed. Wheeling, IL: Harlan Davidson, 2002.

Wilkins, David E. *American Indian Sovereignty and the U.S. Supreme Court: The Masking of Justice.* Austin: University of Texas Press, 1997.

Women

Basch, Norma. *In the Eyes of the Law: Women, Marriage, and Property in Nineteenth-Century New York.* Ithaca: Cornell University Press, 1982.

Braude, Ann. *Radical Spirits: Spiritualism and Women's Rights in Nineteenth Century America.* Boston: Beacon Press, 1989.

Breines, Winifred. *The Trouble Between Us: An Uneasy History of White and Black Women in the Feminist Movement.* New York: Oxford University Press, 2006.

Buhle, Mari Jo, and Paul Buhle, eds. *The Concise History of Woman Suffrage: Selections from the Classic Work of Stanton, Anthony, Gage, and Harper.* Urbana: University of Illinois Press, 1978.

Buhle, Mari Jo. *Women and American Socialism, 1870-1920.* Urbana: University of Illinois Press, 1981.

Campbell, Karlyn Kohrs. *Man Cannot Speak for Her: A Critical Study of Early Feminist Rhetoric.* Westport, CT: Greenwood Press, 1989.

Cott, Nancy. *The Grounding of Modern Feminism.* New Haven: Yale University Press, 1987.

DuBois, Ellen C. *Feminism and Suffrage: The Emergence of an Independent Women's Movement in America, 1848-1869.* Ithaca: Cornell University Press, 1978.

―――. *Harriot Stanton Blatch and the Winning of Woman Suffrage.* New Haven: Yale University Press, 1997.

Evans, Sara. *Personal Politics: The Roots of Women's Liberation in the Civil Rights Movement and the New Left.* New York: Knopf, 1979.

Flexner, Eleanor. *Century of Struggle: The Woman's Rights Movement in the United States.* 1959; rev. ed. Cambridge, MA: Belknap Press, 1975.

Gabin, Nancy. *Feminism in the Labor Movement: Women and the United Auto Workers, 1935-1975*. Ithaca: Cornell University Press, 1990.

Giddings, Paula. *When and Where I Enter: The Impact of Black Women on Race and Sex in America*. New York: William Morrow, 1984.

Higgenbotham, Evelyn Brooks. *Righteous Discontent: The Women's Movement in the Black Baptist Church, 1880-1920.* Cambridge, MA: Harvard University Press, 1993.

Hole, Judith and Ellen Levine. *Rebirth of Feminism*. New York: Quadrangle Books, 1971.

Lerner, Gerda. *The Grimke Sisters from South Carolina: Pioneers for Woman's Rights and Abolition*. New York: Schocken, 1966.

Love, Barbara J, ed. *Feminists Who Changed America, 1963-1975*. Urbana: University of Illinois Press, 2006.

Matthews, Glenna. *The Rise of Public Woman: Woman's Power and Woman's Place in the United States, 1630-1970*. New York: Oxford University Press, 1992.

Miller, Page Putnam, ed. *Reclaiming the Past: Landmarks of Women's History*. Bloomington: Indiana University Press, 1992.

Newman, Louise Michele. *White Women's Rights: The Racial Origins of Feminism in the United States*. New York: Oxford University Press, 1999.

Painter, Nell Irvin. *Sojourner Truth: A Life, A Symbol*. New York: W.W. Norton, 1996.

Rosen, Ruth. *The World Split Open: How the Modern Women's Movement Changed America*. New York: Viking Press, 2000.

Rupp, Leila J. and Verta Taylor. *Survival in the Doldrums: The American Women's Rights Movement, 1945 to the 1960s*. New York: Oxford University Press, 1987.

Ryan, Mary. *Women in Public: Between Banners and Ballots, 1825-1880*. Baltimore: Johns Hopkins University Press, 1990.

Scott, Anne Firor and Andrew MacKay. *One Half the People: The Fight for Woman Suffrage*. Urbana: University of Illinois Press, 1975.

Sochen, June, ed. *The New Feminism in Twentieth Century America*. Lexington, MA: D.C. Heath, 1971.

Springer, Kimberly. *Living for the Revolution: Black Feminist Organizations, 1968-1980*. Durham: Duke University Press, 2005.

Swerdlow, Amy. *Women Strike for Peace: Traditional Motherhood and Radical Politics in the 1960s*. Chicago: University of Chicago Press, 1993.

Wheeler, Marjorie Spruill. *New Women of the New South: The Leaders of the Woman Suffrage Movement in the Southern States.* New York: Oxford University Press, 1993.

www.ingramcontent.com/pod-product-compliance
Lightning Source LLC
Chambersburg PA
CBHW081857280526
45789CB00007B/2739